The Laughing
Savior

THE LAUGHING SAVIOR

SAVIOR

The Discovery and Significance of the
Nag Hammadi Gnostic Library

1817

JOHN DART

1976

HARPER & ROW, PUBLISHERS
New York, Hagerstown, San Francisco, London

Quotations from Nag Hammadi texts are from translations of the Coptic Gnostic Library Project of the Institute for Antiquity and Christianity unless otherwise indicated.

Bible quotations are from the Revised Standard Version.

FIRST EDITION

Designed by Patricia Girvin Dunbar

Library of Congress Cataloging in Publication Data

Dart, John, 1936–
  The laughing Savior.
  Bibliography: p.
  Includes index.
  1. Chenoboskion manuscripts. 2. Gnosticism. I. Title.
BT1390.D35 1976   273'.1   75-36749
ISBN 0-06-061692-X

76 77 78 79 80 81 10 9 8 7 6 5 4 3 2 1

to Gloria with love

CONTENTS

ILLUSTRATIONS

ACKNOWLEDGMENTS

The nerve to write a popular book about a scholarly subject comes from journalism training, no doubt, but my work as a religion writer with the *Los Angeles Times* led me specifically to the dramatic, yet little known, story of the Nag Hammadi Gnostic Library.

After writing a few news stories on the Nag Hammadi manuscripts over several years, I realized that fascinating material for a book could be uncovered through more research. The opportunity came during a professional journalism fellowship at Stanford University in 1973–74 funded primarily by the National Endowment for the Humanities.

In my spare time I was able to explore the stacks of Stanford Library for scholarly works on Gnosticism contained in scattered journals and books. My understanding of the period when the Gnostics flourished was aided by my contact with the Religious Studies Department headed by William A. Clebsch. Special thanks are due to Larry Berman, Jerry Irish, and Robert Hamerton-Kelly.

The major facilitator for this book, however, was the Institute for Antiquity and Christianity, part of the Claremont (Calif.) Graduate School. James M. Robinson, the director, and others associated with the institute provided me with English translations of many texts still unpublished at the time.

Robinson and James Brashler, the institute's assistant director, offered detailed comments on the manuscripts. Brashler also wrote a valuable summary of each title in the library for the appendix of this book. Helpful suggestions came from Birger Pearson, George MacRae, Charles Hedrick, and Douglas Parrott, also associated with the institute. Others who aided with comments were Pheme Perkins, Gilles Quispel, and Gershom Scholem.

I am also grateful for the interest in the book shown by my editor, Marie Cantlon, and her useful suggestions on its organization.

Responsibility for the editorial content of this book, however, rests solely with myself. The choice of material for the book, the emphases, and the conclusions are my own.

I reviewed only the literature available in English, so my apologies to Nag Hammadi scholars whose works were not in English.

While working in Ethiopia during the government changes there in 1974–75, Jean Doresse took time through correspondence to provide valuable details for the story of the Nag Hammadi discovery.

Grateful acknowledgment is also given for permission to reprint Saying of Jesus #8, 28, 42, 64, 79, 96, 98, 114, in *The Gospel According To Thomas*, Coptic text established and translated by A. Guillaumont, H.-CH. Puech, G. Quispel, W. Till & Yassah 'ABD Al Masih. Copyright © 1959 E. J. Brill. By permission of Harper & Row, Publishers, Inc.

Two fellow Timesmen helped with the preparation of the illustrations. Patrick Lynch created the map, and Cal Montney printed most of the photographs.

To my wife Gloria and our children, Kim, John, Randall, and Christopher, gratitude for their patience.

INTRODUCTION

Shortly after World War II the secret scriptures of two historically obscure religious sects were discovered in the Middle East. One discovery was the celebrated Dead Sea Scrolls of the Essenes, a Jewish sect that endured until A.D. 68. The other find was the Nag Hammadi Gnostic Library, a collection of fifty-two religious texts written on papyrus sheets cut and bound into book form. Though the library was found near the Upper Nile city of Nag Hammadi (pronounced Nahg Ha-MAH-Dee) in Egypt, the Gnostics who had composed them were widespread in the Mediterranean lands. They were both internal and external rivals of early Christianity, especially in the second century. Called Gnostics by unfriendly critics in the churches, they claimed to have an esoteric *gnosis* (Greek, "knowledge"), far superior to that of other religious and philosophic groups. (The same root is apparent in the word *agnostic*, one who disclaims any knowledge of God, or capability to know.)

From both the Dead Sea Scrolls and the Nag Hammadi Gnostic Library, scholars expected not only to hear those long-dead religious movements finally tell their own stories, but to obtain unparalleled new insights into the formative years of today's Judaism and its giant offspring, Christianity.

The content and significance of the Dead Sea Scrolls was generally known and appreciated by the late 1950s, but the world has had to wait longer for the Gnostic story.

An extraordinary series of mishaps plagued scholars' efforts to get at the bulk of the manuscripts—Egypt's internal political upheaval and wars with Israel, scholarly rivalries, and slow progress in photographing pages at Cairo's Coptic Museum where most of the manuscripts are stored.

Part of the excitement over the Dead Sea Scrolls was stimulated by the discovery of ancient biblical manuscripts accompanying the Essene literature—something that the Gnostic library lacks.

There were other differences suggesting why the one captured scholarly and public imagination and the other did not.

Some early speculation about the scrolls asked whether Jesus had been an Essene, possibly even the unnamed "righteous teacher" mentioned in the scrolls. But later scholarship discounted both suggestions, leaving only more indirect comparisons to be drawn between the withdrawn Essenes of the Qumran desert community and the first bands of Christians.

Specialists looking for new clues to the life of Jesus and the early church knew by the mid-1950s that the Nag Hammadi Gnostic Library contained a large amount of Christian lore —ranging from outright heretical, writings to near-orthodox philosophical speculations and apocryphal stories. The library also contained *The Gospel of Thomas*, a remarkable arrangement of more than one hundred "sayings of Jesus." This text, one of the few translated and published by 1960, prompted curiosity about a "fifth gospel." The potential for wide religious interest may have been cut short by initial critiques which tended to characterize *Thomas* as a Gnostic compilation derived from Mark, Matthew, and Luke.

The speedier public debut of the Essenes (though not all the scrolls had been translated even by the 1970s) has been explained in other ways, too. For example, Israel's government supported the scholars involved, perhaps seeing the political benefits as well as the cultural. Egypt was in the process of great change, at times experiencing damaged relations with Western countries from where most of the interested scholars

NAG HAMMADI AND ENVIRONS

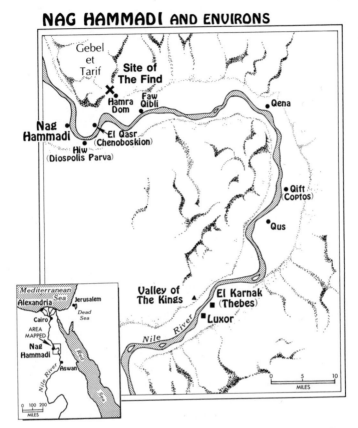

Map of Nag Hammadi and Environs by Patrick Lynch

were coming. Finally, many documents remained in private hands for years before any translations were permitted.

Scholarly interest in the Nag Hammadi library could not be discouraged indefinitely. The collection—actually containing a variety of religious and philosophical treatises, not all "Gnostic"—dates from a period in which much of Western civilization's views of man and morality were shaped.

But can today's Christian culture find any value in the writings of so-called heretics? The Christian church owes much to the Gnostics, religious scholars say. Without the Gnostic crisis, it would have taken longer for the church to form creeds, to select the books to be included in the New Testament, and to give authority to bishops.

The Gnostics sometimes have been credited with producing or provoking the first theological works. "They kept alive the great issues of freedom, redemption and grace, which, after the times of Paul and John, were not adequately discussed by second-century Christian writers," said Robert M. Grant.

At the same time, there was a caustic, bitter strain basic to Gnostic thought. "Gnosticism was the religion that expressed most clearly the mood of defeatism and despair that swept the ancient world in the early centuries of the Christian era," says James M. Robinson of the Claremont Graduate School.

A foretaste of this mood was seen in the Dead Sea Scrolls. The Essenes' apocalyptic writings showed how a people "that had again and again lost its freedom to one world power after another gave up any realistic hope of succeeding in the world," Robinson said.

"Qumran led in part to Nag Hammadi," he wrote, referring especially to religious imagery. "Essene dualism condemned this world with its children of darkness and heralded an apocalyptic deliverance for the sons of light; Gnostic mythology portrayed this world as an evil god's prison for the sparks of the divine, and imparted the knowledge with which they could escape to their lost origin above." This other-worldly escapism was halted in Judaism by orthodox rabbis about A.D. 100, but the trend was not erased from Christianity until two or three centuries later. A Gnostic-like religion, Manichaeism, flourished for a while longer, then faded. A small group of Mandeans living in Iraq are considered the only remnants of the Gnostic faith today.

The modern picture of Gnosticism shaped before the Nag Hammadi discovery was derived primarily from the writings of the second-, third-, and fourth-century Christian leaders. These church fathers wrote polemical pieces against the Gnostics.

And even the neo-Platonic philosopher, Plotinus, joined the anti-Gnostic battle with a work titled, "Against the Gnostics, or Against Those Who Say That the Creator of the World

Is Evil and That the World Is Bad." As Plotinus suggested, the Gnostics had little good to say about the here and now, while Greek philosophy taught that the world reflected order and truth.

The Gnostics believed truth and knowledge, symbolically represented by "light," was linked with a higher God. The lower Creator God and his despoiled world were worthless, and a knowledge of this distinction was the first step toward salvation. The church fathers contended that this attitude led the Gnostics toward amoral behavior in the belief that nothing you do in *this* world matters.

The biblical commandment forbidding the coveting of another's wife was considered "laughable" by the leader of the Carpocratian Gnostics, according to Clement of Alexandria. This sect argued that the Creator God gave men their natural sexual urge toward females, yet commanded each man to keep to his own wife. In the light of this "inconsistency," the Carpocratian men and women would conduct feasts, extinguish the light, and "unite as they will and with whom they will." After they have exercised themselves in fellowship in such a "love-feast," Clement continued sarcastically, the men demand sexual submission from the women by day in keeping with the belief they all belong to one another.

The founder of the Gnostic heresies, or so believed the church fathers, was Simon Magus of Samaria. One of those writing of him, about A.D. 140, was Justin Martyr, himself a Samaritan. Justin said that Simon was from the Samaritan village of Gitta, that he demonstrated magical powers, and that he was worshiped as a god.

Apparently this Simon was the same magician described in the New Testament Book of Acts (8:9–11):

> But there was a man named Simon who had previously practiced magic in the city and amazed the nation of Samaria, saying that he himself was somebody great. They all gave heed to him, from the least to the greatest, saying, "This man is that power of God which is called Great." And they gave heed to him, because for a long time he had amazed them with his magic.

When the apostle Philip came to preach in Samaria, however,

many people believed and were baptized, according to the Book of Acts. "Even Simon himself believed, and after being baptized he continued with Philip. And seeing signs and great miracles performed, he [Simon] was amazed" (Acts 8:13).

The church fathers did not describe the Gnostic Simon as a Christian convert, but as one of history's most outrageous god-pretenders. "He led about with him a certain Helena, whom he had redeemed as a harlot in Tyre, a city of Phoenicia . . ." wrote Irenaeus. "She was his first 'thought,' the mother of all, through whom in the beginning he had conceived the idea of making angels and archangels." This "thought" leaped forward from Simon in his earlier existence as the God of the heavens. She gave birth to the angels and worldly powers which in turn made the world, but those forces detained her because they did not want to be considered merely the products of another being.

Denied her return to her father, and suffering under the powers and angels, "she was shut up in a human body and through the centuries, as from one vessel to another, migrated into ever different female bodies," Irenaeus continued. She was in Helen of Troy, for whom the Trojan War was fought, and continued her ignominious travels from body to body until she ended up in a brothel.

At this point, Simon descended to earth as a man to free his errant "thought" and take her to himself. But since the angels were governing the world badly, he decided to bring things into order. Those humans who recognized Simon as God and who acknowledged Helena as the embodiment of his divine thought were extended "redemption," that is, freedom from the enslaving commandments of those who created the world.

In reality, Irenaeus claimed, Simon's mystery priests lived immorally, practicing exorcisms and erotic magic and concocting love potions.

Simon's pretensions as God led to his eventual downfall, if the account of another church father, Hippolytus, is right. "He said that if he were buried alive he would rise again on the third day," Hippolytus wrote. "Commanding a grave to be dug, he ordered his disciples to heap earth upon him. They did as he commanded, but he remained [in it] until this day. For he was not the Christ."

The image of the Gnostics through the ages has not been entirely one of orgy-justifying mystics. Some Gnostic teachings indicated that their abhorrence for the world led to another reaction—withdrawal from society with its corrupting lusts and greeds. Gnosticism, it has been suggested, encouraged lustful abandon on the one hand and asceticism on the other.

Nevertheless, not all Gnostics felt compelled to live in a radical style. One of the few lengthy Gnostic writings which was preserved by church fathers—and one of the most lucid—is a letter to Flora, apparently a Gnostic initiate, from Ptolemaeus, a Christian Gnostic who frequently quoted Scripture to make his points. He was not willing to condemn the Creator God and conceded that this lower God of the Hebrews was concerned with justice. Ptolemaeus also interpreted the Ten Commandments as pointing toward a reasonable and righteous middle way—neither lustful nor ascetic.

For additional writings by the Gnostics themselves, history had provided little to work with. The British Museum in 1785 acquired manuscripts in Coptic that contained two *Books of Pistis-Sophia*. Two Coptic Gnostic *Books of Jeu* were bought near the ancient Egyptian city of Thebes in 1769 but not recognized for their significance until the late 1800s. These writings, according to Hans Jonas, author of *The Gnostic Religion*, represented "a rather low and degenerate level of gnostic thought" belonging to the declining stage of their speculations.

In reconstructing models of Gnostic belief systems, scholars also examined strains in the surviving manuscripts of the Manichaean religion founded by a religious leader named Mani (A.D. 216–c. 275). Further information was gleaned from old texts of the Mandean sect, from the Egyptian-Greek pagan treatise *Poimandres*, and from some Christian apocryphal writings such as the *Acts of Thomas* which were said to contain Gnostic sections.

Some promise of help came in 1896 when a Coptic codex was purchased in Cairo for the Berlin Museum. It included three Gnostic documents. Unfortunately, these materials still were unpublished by the time of the Nag Hammadi find.

The bulk of the Nag Hammadi texts did not start to become generally available until the mid-1970s. By that time, the significance of the library began to emerge. Two major conclusions were being advanced by scholars closely associated with translating and analyzing the contents:

—Gnosticism may have arisen as a revolt within Judaism. Scholars generally have not considered Simon Magus the originator of the Gnostic movement. Rather a variety of theories have been proposed—some saying the Iranian religious traditions were most influential, others pointing to a wide blending of different religious thought or "an acute Hellenization of Christianity," as one classic nineteenth-century formulation put it. Support has developed for a basic origin near or within Jewish circles despite the virulent attacks against the God of the Jews in the Nag Hammadi books.

—Nag Hammadi may have provided evidence for a theory that Gnostic myths of a heavenly redeemer were around early enough to have influenced the first Christian writers in their descriptions of Jesus' divinity. In other words, the New Testament glorification of Jesus as a preexisting heavenly redeemer who descended to spread saving knowledge, then reascended to heaven, may be indebted in part to the Gnostic idea of a heavenly redeemer.

Both contentions face considerable debate, but, if true, the contemporary understanding of Gnostic impact in the first centuries A.D. is bound to undergo significant alteration.

The Gospel of Thomas, meanwhile, has had improved reviews from some New Testament specialists who believe the Nag Hammadi treatise may, after all, contain authentic sayings of Jesus, some "new" and some older than the New Testament versions.

Gnostic writings also hold appeal for other research. Feminist scholars may find the neglected female side of the deity in numerous Gnostic myths and interpretations. Disciples of Jungian psychology see rich images in Gnostic lore. Mormon church professors are looking for traces of first-century Christian rituals and concepts which they feel were abandoned by the church and restored when the Mormon church was founded.

Gnostic texts, it must be said, are read only with difficulty by the uninitiated. Of course, it was meant to be that way in many cases. Some of the tractates, as they are technically called, were labeled "secret books" by the Gnostics.

Another less tangible but intriguing discovery in the tractates is the mocking laughter in Gnostic myth making. This may be a significant clue to the Gnostic attitude, for it stands in stark contrast to the near absence of laughter, mocking or otherwise, in the New Testament.

But there is more to the Nag Hammadi story than the revelations, myths, and commentaries in the fifty-two papyrus texts. Their contents are matched in intrigue by the struggle to bring the secret books to public light after their discovery in 1945. The difficulties bedeviled a large cast of characters, but the story is best told around a Frenchman who first recognized the significance of the find and an American who doggedly completed the task of making the manuscripts available to all.

PART

I

THE DISCOVERY

ONE

From a Museum
Drawer . . .

A young French graduate student arrived in Cairo in September 1947, excited about examining firsthand the vestiges of ancient Christian monastic life in Egypt. While studying and lecturing in Paris, Jean Doresse had steeped himself in the languages and history of this period. And now the French Institute of Archeology at Cairo had invited him to spend three months exploring for Christian remains in an area three hundred miles south of Cairo in Upper Egypt.

Christianity had put down some of its strongest, earliest roots in Egypt long before the arrival in the seventh century of Islam. Church leaders in Alexandria were voices to contend with as the Christian church developed in the Mediterranean world of the late Roman Empire. The first series of monasteries in the history of Christendom were begun early in the fourth century by monks under St. Pachomius. Born and raised a pagan, Pachomius was said to have become a disciple of the aged hermit Palemon around A.D. 315 to 320. Individual Christian hermits were not uncommon then in Egypt. One of the most popular monks of that period was the venerated St. Anthony.

However, Pachomius eventually sought an alternate style by gathering around him others to form Christian communities along the northern shores of a big bend in the Nile River which begins north of Luxor and completes its swerve near Nag

The ruins of the Basilica of St. Pachomius in the foreground. Doresse originally planned to study the vestiges of the first Christian monastic communities in the region of the Nile. The realization in Cairo that Gnostic manuscripts were discovered in this region led him there for another reason. The discovery site, Gebel et Tarif, is in the background.—Photo, courtesy of Jean Doresse

Hammadi. Innumerable monasteries and convents were started under the influence of Pachomius and his disciples in Egypt. Pachomius' monastic rules later shaped the formation of other religious orders in Christendom.

At first, Jean Doresse's plan to visit the ruins of those monasteries was frustrated. An epidemic of cholera had just hit Egypt that autumn of 1947. Nearly five thousand lives were reported lost in the first month of the disease's spread, mostly in the Nile delta region. Government health measures forced the eager Parisian to postpone his trip to Upper Egypt.

But all was not lost for the tall, slender Frenchman, thirty years old, and his wife, Marianne, who accompanied him. While in Cairo, they had planned to visit the Coptic Museum, a repository of relics from the Coptic period of Egypt. Doresse's wife had met the director of the museum while both were studying

A view of the entrance to the Coptic Museum (left) in old Cairo. Ruins dating from the Roman period are at the right foreground.—The Institute for Antiquity and Christianity

in Paris at the Ecole des Hautes Etudes. Doresse studied Egyptology two years later at the same school and knew of the director's reputation from Marianne and from his professors.

Before traveling to Egypt, "I wrote and received the most friendly answer," Doresse later recalled. "He was anxious to see me but he would not write why. Arriving in Cairo, we went immediately to the Coptic Museum . . ."

Entering the oldest section of the Egyptian capital, they passed by the ruins of a huge tower, part of the remains of a Roman fortified enclosure. A considerable amount of Christian lore is associated with Old Cairo, including the legend that a church there sits on a spot where the infant Jesus was taken by the fleeing Mary and Joseph. The spot is also said to be where the apostle Mark founded the first Christian church in Egypt.

The Coptic Museum, in contrast to its surroundings, appears rather modern. The entrance of the yellow stucco building leads to a pleasant enclosed courtyard enhanced by marble columns and statues. Tourists are directed to the left where two floors of artifacts are gathered into a seemingly endless display of cloth, papyrus, statuary, jewelry, paintings—nearly all relics from the culture of Egyptian Christians known as the Copts.

The Coptic language was developed by Egyptians around the second century A.D., using the alphabet of the widely known Greek language and adding six letters for sounds not found in Greek. Although Coptic was gradually replaced by Arabic as the common tongue in Egypt between the eighth and tenth centuries, the language was preserved in the liturgy of the Coptic Christian church just as Latin continued up to modern times as the liturgical language of the Roman Catholic church. By 1947, the year the Doresses visited Cairo, Coptic was still spoken by some families in the Coptic Christian communities which made up about 8 percent of the Egyptian population.

To the right of the museum's entrance is a wing containing a large reading room with relatively few books. Doresse and his wife headed left to the museum office where they met the director, Togo Mina. A dark-complexioned man of forty-one, Mina was short, about five feet five inches, and his slightly stooped shoulders only emphasized the difference in height with that of the lean Jean Doresse, who was five feet eleven inches. The two men were only eleven years apart in age, but Mina, who suffered from diabetes and other complications, looked much older.

Mina wasted no time in revealing why he was so interested in Doresse's visit to Cairo. "He opened a drawer of his desk, took out of it a voluminous packet, and showed me, in a book-cover of soft leather, some pages of papyrus filled with large, fine Coptic writing . . ." Mina suggested that the documents might date from the third or fourth century A.D.

"He asked me if I could identify the contents of the pages," Doresse said. "From the first few words, I could see that these were Gnostic texts . . ."

One manuscript bore two titles, *The Sacred Book of the Great Invisible Spirit* and *The Gospel of the Egyptians*. This great invisible spirit was described in an opening line as the "Father whose name cannot be uttered," one who came forth from the heights of perfection. The neatly written, ragged-edged text may not have named the unnameable Spirit-Father,

Togo Mina (left) and Jean Doresse study the manuscripts at the Coptic Museum. The Museum director and the Frenchman eventually located two other collections from the Nag Hammadi cache in Cairo but were unable to obtain them before Mina died in 1949.—Photo, courtesy of Jean Doresse

but it went on to identify all sorts of other "powers" and "lights" of the heavens.

The packet's first text was a "secret book" of John, since translated literally *The Apocryphon of John*. The text purported to be the apostle John's account of an appearance by Jesus after his resurrection. After descending as a blazing light from the parted heavens, Jesus told John not only about the array of heavenly powers but also about man's origins according to a bizarre Gnostic version of the Genesis story.

Doresse warmly congratulated Mina on the extraordinary discovery. Altogether the packet contained five treatises. Besides *The Apocryphon of John* and *The Gospel of the Egyp-*

tians, there was *The Dialogue of the Savior,* in which Jesus answered questions from his disciples as well as from a Mary and a Miriamme.

Two other texts resembled each other—*Eugnostos, the Blessed,* basically a non-Christian work in the form of a letter, and *The Sophia of Jesus Christ,* a dialogue between Jesus and his disciples. Unlike Mary or Miriamme, Sophia was not another woman follower of Jesus. Sophia is the Greek term for "wisdom," one of many words the scribes did not translate into Coptic.

Curious about how the Coptic Museum acquired these precious writings, Doresse pressed Mina for details. The museum director happily disclosed that in the previous year a man showed the papyrus manuscripts to George Sobhy, a museum board member who was trying to popularize the use of Coptic language in Egyptian Christian circles. Sobhy sent the man to Togo Mina, who bought the texts for a reportedly modest price on October 4, 1946, nearly a year before the young Frenchman's visit.

Whether Mina sought any expert appraisal in the intervening year is not known, but apparently the museum official was cautious about revealing the manuscripts' existence. Mina knew Doresse had been lecturing in Paris on Coptic Gnostic literature, but Mina's friendly letter to Doresse prior to the visit mentioned nothing about possible new Gnostic texts.

This batch of centuries-old literature, in surprisingly good condition, suddenly opened new doors on the historically obscure Gnostics—those religious rebels of the first few centuries A.D. known then throughout Mediterranean culture. Except through the biased accounts of church leaders who denounced them as heretics, the Gnostics left few testimonies for posterity.

The Apocryphon of John and *The Sophia of Jesus Christ* were among four Coptic papyrus texts found in Egypt in 1896, but more than fifty years later were still not published. A noted German professor, Carl Schmidt, had drawn attention to the find. Excerpts from those writings, which also included the Gnostic *Gospel of Mary* and the Christian apocryphal writing *The Acts of Peter,* appeared in articles around the turn of the century. But full publication of the translations was thwarted in 1912 when a water pipe burst in the printer's cellar and ruined the plates. Schmidt returned to the work periodically and was preparing a new edition from the old proofs shortly before his death in 1938. During World War II the task was eventually entrusted to Walter C. Till, an Austrian scholar.

Now, in the Cairo of 1947, a new cache of Coptic Gnostic scripture surfaced, and Doresse had to reflect on the possibility that his copies of *The Apocryphon of John* and *The Sophia of Jesus Christ* could beat the Till versions into print. It was time for cooperation, however, not oneupmanship. Doresse and Mina decided to invite three other persons to participate in publishing translations of the Coptic Museum's texts. They were Canon Etienne Drioton, the French director general of the Egyptian Department of Antiquities; Henri-Charles Puech of Paris, Doresse's teacher and a professor of the history of religions; and the new editor of the 1896 discovery, Walter Till. Both Till and Doresse would benefit from comparisons of their duplicate texts, noting the differences in footnotes to their respective translations, but as it turned out Doresse's plans were unfulfilled.

TWO

Cairo, Luxor, Jerusalem, and New York

A few days after Doresse had examined the remarkable packet in the director's desk drawer, the ever-cautious Mina asked Doresse if he would like to see more papyrus pages, similar to those they had studied at the museum. These, Mina said, were held by Albert Eid, a Belgian antiquities dealer in Cairo.

Doresse responded happily, and the two men jumped into Mina's car, Mina switching to the dark-tinted glasses he always wore when driving. Eid's shop was in a section called Khan Khalil.

"Eid was good enough to let me look at all the manuscripts he had bought," Doresse said. In appearance and content they resembled the museum's papyri, though these pages were in poorer condition. They were "undoubtedly Gnostic," Doresse concluded. The Frenchman found, among other texts, *The Gospel of Truth* and a letterlike treatise about the resurrection addressed to a Rheginos.

Mina and Doresse left Eid's shop determined to find out where these two sets of manuscripts had been discovered in the hope that yet more could be found at the source. But inquiries along the antiquities grapevine yielded little. "They spoke mysteriously of a large find of manuscripts having been made near a hamlet called Hamra-Dum [Hamra Dom], well to the north of Luxor," Doresse said.

Mina and the Doresses went to Eid's shop again, and Mina told the dealer that the Coptic Museum wanted to buy the manuscripts for a reasonable price. Mina warned Eid he could not allow the documents to leave Egypt. The Belgian agreed to supply Doresse with photographs of the fragile papyrus leaves; if the pages left the country or somehow disappeared, the photos were to be handed over at no cost to the Coptic Museum.

In the course of their dealings, Eid told Mina and Doresse of the possibility that still more codices—a technical name for the leather-bound "books" of papyri—could be found in Cairo. But Eid could not prove it, said Doresse, "so Togo thought that it was one more legend of fabulous discoveries aimed at increasing the price of Eid's codex."

Despite the sketchiness of the rumor about the Gnostic codices being found near a hamlet in Upper Egypt, Doresse felt it was worth checking. Hamra Dom was located in the very area which was the object of Doresse's original mission to Egypt. He reached Upper Egypt by plane, the railway service still being suspended because of the cholera epidemic.

Hoping to hear stories of a large papyrus discovery, Doresse spent long weeks rambling over ruins of Coptic monasteries and remains of earlier Egyptian greatness, the monuments of the Pharoahs. To inquire openly about such a discovery would have invited financial speculation on any items still circulating. "The silence that invariably hides the real circumstances surrounding great finds—and which we had thought we might break—was again impenetrable," he said.

Unknown to Doresse or Mina, or to the rest of the world, about the same time in Jerusalem the significance of another amazing discovery was coming to light. A portion of the now-famous Dead Sea Scrolls had been taken to Jerusalem and Bethlehem by Bedouin tribesmen who had discovered them in caves and sold them to antiquities dealers. It wasn't until November 24, 1947, that the value of the scrolls was recognized. That moment came when archeologist Elazar L. Sukenik of Hebrew University peered through a barbed-wire barrier at an inscribed scrap of leather from one of the scrolls and sensed their antiquity. Tension was high then in Palestine because any day the United Nations was expected to vote on the establishment of a Jewish state. Sections of Jerusalem were divided to keep Arabs and Jews apart, but Sukenik obtained a military pass to keep an appointment to see some scroll fragments.

On November 29, Sukenik and an Armenian friend made a bus trip to Bethlehem to purchase three scrolls; then they rode back to Jerusalem with the scrolls wrapped in paper under their arms. "All around were groups of Arabs, some sullen and silent, others gesticulating wildly," Sukenik wrote in a personal journal. That night the news came that the United Nations had voted to establish Israel, and the predicted protests by groups of Palestinians began.

Months earlier, four other scrolls had come into the possession of a Syrian Orthodox church leader in Jerusalem, Mar Athanasius Y. Samuel. It was not long before Sukenik and Americans William Brownlee and John Trever were in contact with the prelate. Thus began the story of the Dead Sea Scrolls, which in time would be identified as the sacred writings and Bible texts of a Jewish sect called the Essenes.

Like the scrolls, the Coptic Gnostic codices had been discovered earlier by people unaware of their significance. In both cases, it wasn't until the fall of 1947 that a scholar could identify them. Then came the necessary backtracking to find the sources.

Unsuccessful in his trip to the Luxor region, Doresse returned to Cairo in December, only a short time before his three-month mission was to end. "Togo Mina was now definitely persuaded that there was nothing more to be discovered," Doresse said. An announcement of the museum's acquisition was given to the Egyptian press, and Cairo newspapers of January 11 and 12, 1948, carried brief items on the discovery. The news prompted "no great stir in a country so inured to archeological marvels," said Doresse.

Back in Paris, Doresse got together with his professor, Henri-Charles Puech, to write a report for the scholarly world. It was forwarded on February 8 to the prestigious Académie des Inscriptions et Belles-Lettres. Doresse's summary account to the academy, to which Puech "lent his authority," as Doresse put it, aroused a "moderate" degree of interest. Le Monde, a leading French newspaper, ran a three-sentence story on February 23 under the headline, "Discovery of a Papyrus of the Fourth Century":

> The Academy has been informed of the discovery, recently made in Egypt, of a collection on papyrus, of 152 pages, dating from the sixth [*sic*] century of our era. It contains in Coptic translation five unpublished Gnostic books. They furnish interesting information about the beliefs of that time.

Although the news article spoke of only five Gnostic books, Doresse had also mentioned in his academy report the existence of the Eid codex which contained another four or five Gnostic treatises. That was nowhere near the total number of manuscripts that would surface.

Several months into 1948 Doresse received from Cairo some mail with photographs of yet more Coptic texts on papyrus, again Gnostic in content. He appealed for travel funds from the secretary general of the academy and obtained the money in short order.

Arriving in Cairo in October, Doresse met with Miss Marika Dattari, whose father was a noted coin collector. Miss Dattari, in sending the photographs to Paris, had indicated that she was the owner, but representing her in Cairo was Phokion G. Tano, an antiquities dealer who claimed to be her business manager.

Doresse had met Tano before he left Egypt at the end of 1947. Tano advised him to stay longer then because of indications that more manuscripts were around. "I think now," said Doresse years after the episode, "that Tano knew about the other codices, wanted to buy them but didn't have the necessary money, so he had to direct them to another buyer—and associate—Miss Dattari." (Later research was to turn up the fact that two European scholars saw some codices in another antiquities shop as early as March 1946, but they were unable to acquire them.)

Sitting down to scan the Dattari-Tano codices, Doresse found himself before hundreds of papyrus pages held together in the now-familiar soft leather bindings. "I was allowed to make no more than a rapid inspection of them," said Doresse. Air raid warnings, which blared at what seemed to Doresse to be the

The bulk of the Nag Hammadi Gnostic library. Eleven of the 13 codices had leather covers. They are among the earliest examples of bound books ever found.—Photo, courtesy of Jean Doresse

slightest provocation, cut short the few evenings he was permitted to peruse the pages. Egypt had been at war with Israel off and on since May 15 when the Jewish state had officially come into being.

Enthralled by the magnitude of the Dattari-Tano codices, Doresse ran his eyes and fingers over four times as many Gnostic texts as he had already been privileged to see, most of the treatises never before available to historians.

"I went . . . from surprise to astonishment," recalled Doresse. He encountered some "sensationally attractive titles," such as *The Revelation of Adam to His Son Seth* (later named simply *The Apocalypse of Adam*), *The Letter of Peter to Philip*, *The Gospel of Philip*, and *The Gospel of Thomas*. The "gospels" of Philip and Thomas were unlike the four New Testament gospels since they didn't concern themselves with a narrative of the life and death of Jesus. *The Gospel of Philip* appeared to Doresse to be a rambling treatise consisting of "lofty speculations." *The Gospel of Thomas* strung together a series of seemingly unconnected sayings of Jesus. It began:

> Here are the secret words which Jesus the Living spoke, and which Didymus Judas Thomas wrote down.
> And he said: Whoever penetrates the meaning of these words will not taste death!
> Jesus says: Let him who seeks not cease to seek until he finds. When he finds he will be astonished; and when he is astonished he will wonder, and will reign over the universe!

Doresse could see that penetrating the meaning of the one hundred fourteen sayings would be difficult because of the cryptic nature of many passages. Nonetheless, much of the "gospel" went over familiar ground—parables about the lost sheep, the pearl, new wine in old wineskins, and the mustard seed, for instance. The *Thomas* versions nearly always varied from Matthew, Mark, or Luke, but then even the New Testament gospel accounts differed among themselves. Saying No. 100, for example, is much shorter and ends differently than the "tribute to Caesar" stories in Matthew (22:15–22), Mark (12:13–17), and Luke (20:20–26): "They showed Jesus a gold piece and said to him, 'Caesar's men demand taxes from us.' He said to them, 'Give to Caesar what belongs to Caesar, give to God what belongs to God, and give to me what is mine.'"

The Gospel of Thomas seemed destined to be the most spectacular book in the Coptic Gnostic collection—now by all appearances a "library," containing various kinds of writings and at least several non-Gnostic works. That such a library of fifty-two treatises should have existed centuries ago was not surprising, but that it should turn up relatively intact after so long was spectacular in terms of archeological discoveries. The great majority of texts were previously unknown to scholars. It would soon be determined that some Greek papyrus found in Egypt around the turn of the twentieth century had a few sayings of Jesus that matched those in *The Gospel of Thomas*, but the latter was the first complete copy ever found. Remarkably, *Thomas'* form was like the presumed style of the never-found "Q" document which scholars think was used by Matthew and Luke (the Gospels of John and Mark having relied on other sources).

Codex II, a part of the Nag Hammadi library inaccessible for study until 1956, is held open to show its book form. Later the papyrus sheets were cut down the middle to place each page between sheets of plexiglass for preservation.— Photo, courtesy of Jean Doresse

Doresse undoubtedly could have captured worldwide attention by announcing the discovery of a "fifth gospel," but common sense and ordinary scruples were enough to encourage him to proceed with quiet care. Such an announcement would have put the manuscripts out of reach financially for the Coptic Museum, or any reputable scholarly agency, and would have prolonged the opportunity to translate them. Announcing another gospel would be meaningless without a decent description of its contents, something that Doresse had no chance to do as yet.

Scholars know only too well that careful study and comparison of such documents can produce unforeseen results. The

Gnostic library was too large to say immediately that *The Gospel of Thomas* would be the most important treatise to emerge from the collection.

Mina and Doresse began the touchy matter of negotiating to buy the Dattari-Tano collection. The situation was touchy because the Egyptian government then had a tendency to take the legal expedient of confiscating historical treasures rather than paying a fair price, said Doresse. The practice was so common that few owners of a valuable antiquity, however legitimately acquired, offered it to the government. They preferred instead to export it and sell it on the clandestine market.

Mina secured the promise of some government funds, but bargaining with the Dattari-Tano team was postponed when political unrest in Cairo brought national affairs to a halt. Prime Minister Nokrashi Pasha was assassinated on December 28, 1948, by a member of the Moslem Brotherhood, a group Pasha had ordered suppressed the month before. The Coptic Museum would have to await the formation of a new government.

That wasn't the first setback of the winter of 1948–49. Another set of Gnostic texts slipped from the museum's grasp.

Eid had taken his papyri to New York City, looking for a market. The Belgian antiquities dealer earlier bragged to Doresse and Mina that he planned to smuggle out the Gnostic pages, claiming the administrative controls on export of antiquities then "were completely inefficient." When leaving the country, Eid showed the Antiquities Department an assortment of carved figures, coins, manuscripts, and other items he planned to sell in the United States—nothing Egyptian authorities would insist on keeping in the country, according to Doresse. Eid may have figured a way to slip the Gnostic papyri into a box at the last minute before it was nailed shut by the authorities, conjectured Doresse. "Anyhow, he told everyone afterward that the thing was so easy to do!" said Doresse.

Eid approached the Bollingen Foundation in New York with *The Gospel of Truth* and other texts in hand. He asked twelve thousand dollars, saying he was already offered a sum by the University of Michigan. The university, known in the Cairo antiquities market for its papyrus collection, was contacted by Eid from New York in January 1949.

Neither the university nor the foundation was able to give Eid what he wanted. The foundation, established by philanthropist Paul Mellon only three years earlier, had excited academic circles because of its attractive purpose: to assist scholarly research and publication of books deemed too costly by other publishers. Its particular interests included comparative religion, symbolism, mythology, philosophy, and archeology. John D. Barrett, a Bollingen official, told Eid that the foundation did not normally buy ancient manuscripts.

Failing to obtain a U.S. buyer, Eid asked the foundation to keep his collection in its safe. That request was refused, and a frustrated Albert Eid left for Europe by way of Cairo.

The connection between Eid and the Bollingen Foundation was instigated by Gilles Quispel, a Dutch authority in philology and early church history. Quispel had been studying the second-century Gnostic thinker Valentinus when he read of Doresse's reports of the Gnostic papyri in the spring of 1948. Doresse was later questioned by Quispel in person about the Valentinian content of Eid's codex. That summer Quispel urged the New York foundation to buy the writings if they became available, and Mellon himself interviewed Doresse about the manuscripts. Word got to Eid of this possible buyer, apparently through Doresse.

But after Eid's abortive trip to the United States, Quispel lost track of Eid in the early months of 1949. "The situation was extremely delicate," said the Dutch scholar. "The rumor went round—which later turned out to be correct—that its owner had died. It was not known where the codex was to be found, what it contained and who was its new owner." It would not be the first time that such a collector's item had disappeared entirely from the market, noted Quispel.

Meanwhile, precautions were being taken in Cairo to safeguard the approximately forty texts owned by Miss Dattari and Tano. The museum board authorized a search for funds, but it was decided that until the money could be raised, Doresse would make a complete inventory of the books, then deposit them, in escrow, as it were, at the Department of Antiquities.

The valuable manuscripts were placed unceremoniously in a suitcase, indicative of the feeling then that this was merely a temporary action. Little could the principals have suspected that the documents would sit in the suitcase for the next seven years. The inaccessibility ended only after the government declared such writings national property and a lawsuit by the owners seeking full compensation failed.

For a while in 1949, however, it looked like Tano and Miss Dattari would receive their fair price. A new government had formed in February. The minister of public instruction was about to allocate something around forty thousand to fifty thousand Egyptian pounds to the Coptic Museum when that government also fell on July 25.

THREE

The Jesus Curse

The repeated disappointments were taking their toll on the museum director. Sick for several months, Mina died in October 1949 at the age of forty-three. Doresse was convinced that the delays contributed to his death. He recalled Mina's "anguish" one day when it was learned that the government was postponing an important decision.

The demise of Mina and Eid . . . the disappearance of one set of manuscripts in Europe . . . a suitcase of papyrus texts sealed by government inaction in Cairo—all these were misfortunes and obstacles to revealing the sacred secrets of the Gnostics. They prompted Doresse to wonder: Were commercial and academic covetousness and political instability the only deterrents?

Were the troubles due instead to the "maledictions that the Egyptian Gnostics had written out in full upon their works against anyone gaining unlawful knowledge of them"? Several Gnostic works described themselves as "secret" and "hidden" mysteries, but *The Apocryphon of John* contained a specific warning of a "curse." Near the text's conclusion, Jesus says in his discourse with John:

> "For truly I have given these things to you to write them down, and they shall be put in a safe place." Then he said to

me, "Cursed is everyone who shall impart these things for a gift, or for food, or for drink, or for clothing, or for anything resembling these."

This malediction, of course, appears also at the end of the Berlin Museum's copy of the *Apocryphon* which had defied publication for a half-century.

Doresse was aware in his musings that Upper Egypt, reputedly the area where the Gnostic manuscripts were found, was the focus of public fascination in the 1920s and 1930s over the so-called "Pharaoh's curse." The tomb of King Tutankhamen, who died about 1,335 B.C., was discovered in 1922 across the Nile River from Luxor. The tomb's remarkable secret compartments, each yielding gold and silver treasures, generated enormous worldwide curiosity. During a three-month period in 1926, an estimated 12,300 tourists visited the tomb in the Valley of the Kings where a series of Pharaonic tombs had been found over the years.

But during the decade following the unsealing of the tomb of King Tut, as he became popularly known, more than twenty persons said to be connected with that expedition died. The first such "victim" was Lord Carnarvon, the supervisor of the excavation, who died April 6, 1923, after three weeks' illness from a mosquito bite. News reports later heralded the "third victim," the "fourth victim," and so on. Some deaths appeared to be quite unusual; others were rather unremarkable, but talk about the effects of the curse persisted. It was said to have wording such as: "Death will come on swift pinions to those who disturb the rest of the Pharaoh."

By 1933, however, a German Egyptologist debunked the Pharaoh's curse story on at least two points: (1) Some "victims" on the lists were entirely unrelated to the tomb expedition, and (2) no such curse was ever found inscribed in or around the tomb.

Howard Carter, the Britisher who was the principal archeologist and discoverer, attributed the speculations on the one hand to a "form of literary amusement" and on the other to "the foolish superstitions which are far too prevalent among emotional people in search of 'psychic' excitement." Carter himself died in London in 1939 at about the age of sixty-six.

Doresse alluded to the Gnostic warning against revealing their secrets in the introduction to his book, *The Secret Books of the Egyptian Gnostics*, published in English in 1960. (By that time, some of the Gnostic essays were being published, and the list of deaths had not expanded beyond Eid and Mina.)

The "curse" of Jesus in *The Apocryphon of John*, put into Jesus' mouth by Gnostic authors, followed a time-honored practice of mystic groups warning their members that such sacred scriptures should not fall into the wrong hands.

For modern man, to whom the message was not addressed, much more interesting is the preceding sentence in which Jesus advises putting the writings in a safe place. In the case of the Gnostic papyri, the place, wherever it was, had been "safe" for centuries.

Where was the Gnostic library hidden? wondered Doresse. A tomb, pagan or Christian? In the ruins of a house or monastic building? How old were they? Under what circumstances could they have been buried?

In Israel, by 1949, comparable questions were already being answered about the Dead Sea Scrolls. A cave that had contained some of the scrolls was found sixteen miles east of Jerusalem in cliffs overlooking the Dead Sea. Nearby was Khirbet Qumran, Arabic for "the ruins of Qumran." The ruins had never been systematically excavated, but the site was explored in 1949. Uncovering the Essene "monastery" was only a matter of time.

Meanwhile, in Egypt the political situation was improving considerably, encouraging Doresse to plan another trip to the rumored location of the Gnostic discoveries. On January 3, 1950, the Wafd party won a big majority in elections, and the leader of the party, Mustafa el Nahas Pasha, became the new prime minister. On January 16, amid widespread political optimism, King Farouk and Prime Minister Pasha drove through the streets of Cairo to open the Egyptian Parliament. In his speech from the throne, the rotund monarch pledged his country's loyalty to the aims of the United Nations and to those of the Arab people. King Farouk promised attention to improved social conditions, education, and employment.

In this atmosphere Doresse left Cairo late that month to find some answers in Upper Egypt. Bits of information collected by Doresse indicated the papyri were discovered near the village of

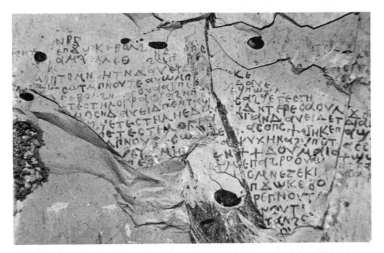

The wall of a cave in the side of Gebel et Tarif where a monk once painted in the Coptic language the beginnings of Old Testament Psalms.—Photo courtesy of James M. Robinson.

Hamra Dom. That would place the alleged discovery site near the ancient settlement of Chenoboskion by the cliffs of Gebel et Tarif. The ruins of the Basilica of St. Pachomius lay several miles to the east, but Doresse was looking for signs of ancient "enemies" of the church whose writings were bound to tell more about early Christianity than his study of monastery sites ever could have produced.

Doresse and his wife traveled to the area on the pretext of inspecting any ancient remains of note. With his moustache, pith helmet, white scarf, and sport coat, Doresse looked very much the part of a European adventure-seeker. He and his wife feigned "deepest curiosity" in several Pharaonic tombs of the Sixth Dynasty located halfway up the eastern face of Gebel et Tarif. Pillagers had long ago robbed the tombs of any obvious relics. The caves were accessible because rock debris formed slopes halfway up the cliffs at some spots. Approaching the series of caves from the south, the Doresses were shown the first cave known for its wall writings in red paint. They were the beginnings, in Coptic, of Psalms 51 through 93, possibly the writing of a Christian monk. In caves further to the north they were shown Greek invocations to Zeus Sarapis. Below the caves for some two hundred yards lay a strip of barren, sandy ground which, Doresse was told, was once a Greco-Roman cemetery.

The European couple was led by the peasant guides "of their own initiative to the southern part of the cemetery and [they] showed us a row of shapeless cavities," said Doresse. In one of these holes, they said, some peasants from Hamra Dom and environs were digging for nitrate-rich soil called *sebakh* when they found a large jar filled with leaves of papyrus, bound together like books. The jar was broken, and a Coptic priest was summoned from a nearby village. He tried to read them, but couldn't, being familiar only with the Coptic of his church's liturgy. The villager had little reason to assume they were important.

Doresse heard a report that some peasants burned a few pages to heat their tea, but that was never confirmed. The peasants, it was also said, divided up the treasure, some selling their portions for a mere three Egyptian pounds to middlemen who took them to Cairo in batches to offer on the antiquities market. Albert Eid, it turns out, bought his manuscript from a Nag Hammadi cereal merchant.

Although more details about the discovery would be learned twenty-five years later, there has never been doubt that information about the container was correct. The ancient use of jars to store manuscripts was known. The Dead Sea Scrolls—believed to date from the second century B.C. and thereafter—were found in large pottery jars.

Doresse was able to learn only that the jar was found in either 1945 or 1946. Later, it was determined that some texts were seen in Cairo as early as March 1946. More persistent interviewing of villagers has since put the time of discovery in the fall of 1945.

A more difficult dating problem, given the lapse of centuries, was when the manuscripts were hidden. Versed in Coptic Christian history and the monastic beginnings of that region of Egypt, Doresse could piece together the events of the fourth century for a possible answer. The biographies of monastery-founder Pachomius, who died about 348, did not mention any

struggles with Gnostics. But in 367, Theodorus, one of Pachomius' successors, ordered that a Lenten letter issued by Bishop
Athanasius of Alexandria be translated into Coptic and read in
all the monasteries. Athanasius' letter listed what were to be the
church-recognized books of the Old and New Testaments. In
enumerating the canonical books, Athanasius also denounced
heretical books which he said were composed to sound as if
they were written centuries earlier by the apostles.

This authoritative letter from Alexandria could have provided the opportunity monastic leaders had sought to order the
destruction of all unorthodox books. Doresse said that the
Theodorus who dictated the wide reading of the letter may
have been the same Theodorus who once deplored a heretical
book which said that "after Eve was deceived and had eaten
the fruit of the tree, it was of the devil that she gave birth to
Cain." This comes close to characterizing some passages in *The
Apocryphon of John,* a book which appears in three copies in
the Gnostic library.

That reconstruction of a possible situation in the late fourth
century is hardly conclusive, but other evidence points to that
period as well. Dates were found—not in the manuscripts, but
on scraps of papyrus stuffed into the covers of the volumes.
These scraps, used to stiffen the covers, included receipts and
other items bearing dates ranging from A.D. 333 to 348.

Thus, the manuscripts were probably bound into book form
about 350 and may have been hidden in the jar in 367, or as
late as 400.

The stories are older. For one thing, scholars are confident
that the narratives were translated from the Greek originals
because of the sometimes poor renditions into Coptic of passages which were probably smoother in the equivalent Greek.
Also, Greek was the more likely original language because of its
widespread use in the Hellenistic age.

The texts are undoubtedly copies rather than original translations. One scribe noted on a page of papyrus between two
treatises: "I have copied this one treatise only, for it was among
a great many that have come into my hands." He had not copied
others, the scribe added, thinking it would have been burden-
some.

Assigning estimated dates of composition to each Gnostic

"gospel," "apocryphon," "treatise," and "apocalypse" awaits the analyses of scholars in years to come, using methods of literary and historical comparison. Some of the writings no doubt date back into the second century when church father Irenaeus was composing tracts against the Gnostics and cited a Gnostic text similar to *The Apocryphon of John*.

For Doresse, who now had photographs of the tall, rugged Gebel et Tarif and the probable discovery site, the find was of extraordinary importance for archeological reasons alone—one of the most "voluminous" and "precious" libraries of papyrus writings ever found.

Doresse was soon to exult in an illustrated article for the U.S. journal *Archeology:* "The number of codices, the care given to their binding and in particular the ancient techniques of these bindings, and the beauty of the different hands establish it as the most remarkable ancient library we possess; there does not exist, even in Greek papyri, anything comparable." Indeed, these were crafted not long after the invention of the codex, a book form as opposed to the rolled scroll. The leather bindings from the Gnostic library are among the oldest ever to survive.

Though Doresse would attach the ancient place name of Chenoboskion to the discovery in future references, later scholars linked the library with the nearest modern town of any size, Nag Hammadi.

In fact, during their fruitful January 1950 visit Doresse and his wife had been the guests of the director of a large Nag Hammadi sugar factory. Preparing to leave Nag Hammadi and eager to share the information about the discovery site, Doresse inquired whether there was a faster route back to their camp adjacent to the Valley of the Kings and across the river from Luxor, the major departure point from Upper Egypt. The Doresses had driven to Nag Hammadi in an old canvas-top Italian car built especially for a Mussolini general in World War II and captured by the British. But the route was long (125 miles) and circuitous, following the winding eastern bank of the Nile most of the way.

Employees at the sugar factory told him there was a way to travel to the Valley of the Kings staying always on the western side of the Nile. There was only about ten miles of flat

Jean Doresse (third from left) and his party of guides who led him to an area at the foot of Gebel et Tarif (in background) where they said the manuscripts were found. Nag Hammadi is about 10 miles southwest of the discovery site.—Photo courtesy of Jean Doresse

desert to cross at one point where the road ended. "It was then a question not of a full day, but of a few hours to get from Nag Hammadi to our camp," said Doresse. "We started after lunch without haste on the road on the west bank of the Nile."

They picked up a peasant guide at a hamlet near the stretch of desert they had to cross. The guide assured them it was easy to get to the Pharaonic temple site of Dandara where the road resumed.

"Yes, it would have been easy with a camel," Doresse recalled, "but the man had no idea of the limited possibilities of a car. We started driving through something comparable to a thoroughly bombed field for one hour before the petrol pump of the car began leaking."

Doresse repaired the pump several times, advancing slowly until darkness made it impossible to fix the leaks. "The pylons of the temple of Dandara were in the distance. We left the car and proceeded on foot, with myself running ahead of my wife and the so-called guide." On the way, Doresse encountered a Bedouin hamlet where a pack of dogs nipped at his trousers, tearing his skin and drawing blood with some bites.

But arriving at the Dandara temple, they found immediate help from a professor who was encamped there on a project to copy down inscriptions. The next morning, Doresse improvised a makeshift fuel supply to the carburetor, and the car made it easily to their camp.

Since Doresse had no chance to have the dog or dogs that bit him examined for rabies, he had to return to Cairo to begin anti-rabies injections. If Doresse had taken the "Jesus curse" seriously, he might have associated his bad luck with acquiring information about the hiding place of the Gnostic library.

If Doresse worried, it was not apparent in his later recollections of the episode: He received daily injections of a "medicine which looked like tepid butter" for one month, but the shots did not produce so much pain as exceptional itching. The Rabies Institute in Cairo was "perfectly managed," and in fact Doresse found that Cairo at that time of the year was "an agreeable town with plenty of intellectual, artistic and gastronomical possibilities."

Events moved slowly after the excitement of the early weeks of 1950. A successor to Togo Mina wasn't named until 1951—one Pahor Labib. The suitcase containing the voluminous Dattari-Tano manuscripts was transferred from the Antiquities Department to the Coptic Museum on June 9, 1952, but the luggage remained sealed.

Political turmoil broke out again in Cairo that summer. Anglo-Egyptian relations had worsened, and nationalist feelings were on the rise. Administration changes by King Farouk never seemed to bring lasting satisfaction. After two more leadership changes in July, a coup d'etat was staged by army officers on the night of July 23, 1952, under the direction of Maj. Gen. Mohammed Naguib. The group included two future prime ministers, Cols. Gamal Abdul Nasser and Anwar Sadat. The new military leaders demanded and got a new regime and the abdication of King Farouk.

The revolution had sweeping effects on Egyptian institutions.

The Department of Antiquities, which had been under French direction since Napoleon's invasion of Egypt, was reorganized. Canon Drioton was dismissed, and an Egyptian director was named in his place.

During all his Gnostic-related adventures in Egypt, Doresse never abandoned his original desires to study vestiges of early Christian monastic life. One of his study trips took him to two Coptic monasteries in the desert near the Red Sea. But the Frenchman was growing increasingly disenchanted with progress, or lack of it, on the study of the Gnostic manuscripts. Translation plans with Puech for the Coptic Museum's codex never got going, in part because of friction between Puech and his student. To some extent, Doresse, who lacked a doctorate then, was at a disadvantage in securing the respect and cooperation of eminent scholars back in Europe.

Nothing seemed to go according to plan. Photographs taken by Doresse of the Eid Codex were given to the Coptic Museum after those pages had been spirited out of Egypt, but the photographs somehow disappeared from the director's office after Mina's death. Doresse, who left Egypt in February 1953 to take an archeological appointment in Ethiopia, mailed another set of photographs of the Eid Codex to the museum, "but it seems that it was lost again!" he said.

Many years later Doresse recalled that he worried little about the kind of "curse" associated with either King Tut's tomb or the Nag Hammadi Gnostic Library. "As for the difficulties in 1949 and in the following years," said Doresse, "the true 'curses' were in fact the 'curses' emanating from antique dealers and from scholars, each of them against his colleagues. If I rather liked to be far from my discovery, it was due to this kind of malediction."

FOUR

The Jung Codex

On a Sunday afternoon, November 15, 1953, in Zurich, Switzerland, an announcement was made to the press concerning a set of manuscripts "presented" publicly to the famous seventy-eight-year-old psychoanalyst Carl Gustav Jung.

The London *Times* published a six-hundred-word article the next day under the headline, "New Light on a Coptic Codex." The news story, filed by an unnamed correspondent, began:

> The contents of a codex of four Coptic Christian writings attributed to the second century A.D., which were acquired last year by the Jung Institute for Analytical Psychology in Zurich, were described at a Press conference here this afternoon, when the papyri under the title Codex Jung, were presented to Professor Jung, founder of the institute.
>
> The codex contains a heretical fifth Gospel and it is believed by the institute that the manuscripts will have outstanding importance for the study of early Christian doctrine and relations between Gnosticism, Judaism and Christianity.
>
> The occasion was one of legitimate self-congratulation by the institute because, but for the pertinacity of its experts and the good fortune of finding a financial backer in Switzerland at the right moment, there might have been no Codex Jung here. The long and delicate negotiations to acquire the manuscripts were

described by Professor Gilles Quispel, of the University of Utrecht, and Professor H. Puech, of the College de France . . .

The article went on to summarize the find near Nag Hammadi, Eid's travels, the institute's acquisition, and an assessment that *The Gospel of Truth* and another tractate in the codex were authored by Valentinus, the second-century Gnostic teacher.

Thus did Eid's codex resurface publicly and acquire the name of its famous recipient.

After Quispel lost track of the codex following Eid's death in 1949, efforts were still being made to interest the Bollingen Foundation in buying the papyri should they be relocated. Even Jung himself wrote to New York, urging the purchase. C. A. Meier of the Jung Institute eventually learned through diplomatic contacts that the codex was sitting in a Brussels safety deposit box. In the summer of 1951 Meier was able to track down the address of the new owner, Simone Eid, widow of the dealer. The parties agreed at an August meeting that the Bollingen Foundation would be asked to buy the writings. The purchase was dependent on Quispel's examination of the papyri to verify their genuineness, and particularly to see if they were Valentinian.

Typical of the slow proceedings, the examination did not occur until seven months later. "Although it was not possible to unpack the papyri," Quispel said, "and such indeed was not justified because of the dilettante way in which they had been packed up, the reading of a single page convinced me that it was Valentinian." Quispel recommended buying them, but Mrs. Eid suddenly asked for a delay, and the New York foundation made some stipulations about furnishing the money that seemed certain to slow matters more. "It appeared as if our exertions spread over four years had all come to nothing," said Quispel.

At that point, Meier decided to phone an American businessman, George H. Page, living in the Zurich suburb of Wallisellen. Page promised to provide the money—thirty-five thousand Swiss francs—in an act later announced to the press as "one of generosity without parallel in the annals of knowledge."

The purchase was completed on May 10, 1952, when Quispel appeared at a Brussels cafe two hours late because he had missed a train connection. He turned the check over to a middleman and was handed the manuscripts. At the request of Mrs. Eid the transaction was not made public for eighteen months for reasons still unexplained.

Though the persistence of the Jung Institute and the presentation to Jung might have seemed surprising to outsiders, the actions would not have been to the admirers of the psychoanalyst. Jung made a serious study of the Gnostics from 1916 to 1926, attracted by what he saw as the Gnostic writers' confrontations with "the primal world of the unconscious." He ended that effort with an unsatisfied feeling, largely because of the paucity of accounts, stemming mostly from the Gnostic opponents, the church fathers. And Jung believed the Gnostics too remote in time, without any psychohistorical link to the present. Only later, by his own account, through his study of the mystical alchemists of the Middle Ages did he find what he considered a bridge between Gnosticism and "the modern psychology of the unconscious."

Jung credited Sigmund Freud with introducing the classical Gnostic motif of the wicked paternal authority into modern psychology. The evil Creator God of the Gnostics "reappeared in the Freudian myth of the primal father and the gloomy superego deriving from that father," Jung said. "In Freud's myth he became a demon who created a world of disappointments, illusions and suffering."

Missing from Freud's system, Jung said, was another essential aspect of Gnosticism—the primordial feminine spirit from another, higher god who gave humans the possibility of spiritual transformation. Writing this shortly after Pope Pius XII issued a 1950 papal bull on the Assumption of the Blessed Virgin Mary, Jung applauded the church for its partial recognition of the feminine aspect of divinity. He said in effect that the bull affirmed that Mary as the Bride is united with the Son in the heavenly bridal chamber, and as Sophia (Wisdom) she is united with the Godhead.

Through their myth making many Gnostics showed themselves to be "not so much heretics as theologians," or even "psychologists," asserted Jung. For example, Jung said, the position of respect given by some Gnostic groups to the snake was not as strange as one might think. The snake represents the

*Carl G. Jung, who took an interest in Gnosticism from
1916 to 1926, termed Gnostics "psychologists," and again as
"not so much heretics as theologians." The psychologist was
presented with parts of Codex I in the 1950's, the only part
of the Nag Hammadi library to leave Egypt. Photo by
Ruth Bailey, courtesy of Princeton University Press.*

"extra-human quality in man," he said. The cold-blooded, star-
ing serpent expresses man's fear of the inhuman "and his awe
of the sublime, of what is beyond human ken."

Jung found important symbolism in a lurid Christian-Gnos-
tic story recounted by fourth-century church father Epiphanius from a Gnostic text called *The Great Questions of Mary*
(not found in the Nag Hammadi library). In the story, Jesus is
said to have taken Mary onto a mountain where he produced a
woman from his side and began to have intercourse with her.
Eating his own flowing semen, he said that this was to be done
that we might have life.

Mary was so shocked she sank to the ground.

Raising her up, Jesus asked, "Why do you doubt me, o you of little faith?"

Jesus' subsequent remarks were sayings borrowed from the Gospel of John, including, "If I have told you earthly things and you do not believe, how can you believe if I tell you heavenly things?" (John 3:12) and ". . . unless you eat the flesh of the Son of man and drink his blood, you have no life in you" (John 6:53).

Jung said that the mountain represented the place of spiritual ascent and revelation, a well-known mythical motif. Christ symbolized the epitome of man, particularly the "second Adam." Adam, of course, received Eve, his conjugal mate, from his side, according to Genesis. "Just as Adam, before the creation of Eve, was supposed by various traditions to be male/female, so Christ here demonstrates his androgyny in a drastic way," Jung said.

Taken literally, the story would be as offensive to third- and fourth-century tastes as to those today, Jung wrote. "For the medical psychologist there is nothing very lurid about it," he added. Such "shocking" images can appear in dreams or during psychological treatment. By quoting John 3:12, said Jung, the episode's author was saying the vision was to be understood symbolically. The eating of semen, Jung suggested, may have been symbolic of Christ as the inner man who is reached by the path of self-knowledge—"the kingdom of heaven is within you."

Although Jung was "presented" with the Nag Hammadi codex taken illegally out of Egypt, Page stipulated that it be returned to Cairo eventually. That was probably an inevitable arrangement because the Jung Codex was only partially intact. Of five titles, only *The Apocryphon of James* and *The Treatise on the Resurrection* were complete. About forty missing pages were in the Dattari-Tano collection sitting in the Coptic Museum.

Agreements were reached to return the Jung Codex pages to Cairo once the scholarly work was done. (The last pages were sent to the museum in 1975 following the publication of the last section of translations.) In turn, Quispel was permitted to transcribe the rest of the pages at the museum on April 2, 1955. Watching the ropes binding the luggage being untied, the seals broken, and small boxes of papyri opened amidst "the noise of a spray can used to kill the ants," Quispel found the missing pages on top, mixed up and many of them fragmentary.

In that same year, some of the Gnostic writings were beginning to appear in print. The Gnostic treatises discovered in 1896 were finally published in Germany by Walter Till, who had been granted access to the Nag Hammadi versions of *The Apocryphon of John* and *The Sophia of Jesus Christ* for footnote comparisons. Also in 1955, Quispel, Puech, and C. W. Van Unnik described the Jung Codex in a book of that title.

Activity in Egypt picked up in 1956. Pahor Labib, the director of the Coptic Museum, published page photographs from much of Codex I and parts of Codex II, including *The Gospel of Thomas, The Gospel of Philip,* and *The Nature of the Archons.* The Egyptian government confirmed the worst fears of Tano and Miss Dattari by declaring the suitcase collection to be national property and making a token payment to the owners.

An international committee of ten persons was appointed to publish a standardized edition of the library. Quispel and Puech, accompanied by Antoine Guillaumont of France, were the only foreigners attending the long first committee meeting in Cairo that lasted from late September to the end of October.

Elaborate plans were laid, but the political situation gave a foreboding of more interruptions. The two French scholars, Puech and Guillaumont, left Cairo just as the Suez Canal crisis was breaking at the end of October, a conflict that brought French and British troops onto Egyptian soil. Quispel, lingering until the last moment, finally left Egypt on an American ship in early November.

FIVE

The Straits of Scholarship

From their hotel or on walks to the university, the assembled professors could squint against the April morning sunlight toward the geographical toe of Italy's boot just a few miles away. In the city of Messina, on the northeastern tip of Sicily, sixty-nine men and women from eleven countries gathered in 1966 for a conference that was the first of its kind—the International Colloquium on the Origins of Gnosticism.

The academic mix included not only scholars involved in biblical and early church studies but also those interested in the histories of religions and comparative religious studies. Such a meeting was made possible, of course, by the earthenware "time capsule" discovered in the sands of Egypt some twenty years earlier.

Responding to a broadly felt need for academic orientation in a field of study waiting to be recultivated, Ugo Bianchi and his colleagues at the University of Messina arranged the unique six-day colloquium in collaboration with the International Association for the History of Religions.

Even before they arrived for the April 13 opening, most participants had a good idea of what was going to be said. Organizers persuaded most of the delegates (including sixteen who could not come) to mail in advance their papers, which were mimeographed and distributed to other delegates.

Swamped with reading material, one contributor remarked,

"I received five kilograms [eleven pounds] of material, but I had only time to read four kilograms." Only four papers were scheduled to be read in full, leaving time and energy for discussions and enjoyment of the Sicilian setting.

With so many professors versed in the tales of antiquity, the myths of Scylla and Charybdis kept cropping up in conversations. Scylla and Charybdis were female monsters of Greek mythology who lurked in the Straits of Messina for foolhardy navigators attempting to pass through. The once-beautiful Scylla was a six-headed ogre who would snatch men from the decks of passing ships. Charybdis used whirlpool action at the other end of the straits to suck in seawater and take along with it any passing ships. Odysseus, in his travels, narrowly escaped death at the two-mile-wide northern strait guarded by Charybdis.

When the opening paper of the colloquium was read, however, it was not Greek mythology but Iranian mythology that was the prime topic of discussion. Geo Widengren of Uppsala, Sweden, president of the International Association for the History of Religions, vigorously championed his thesis that the origins of Gnosticism could be found in the Persian religions such as Zoroastrianism with their dualistic tendencies.

Iranian explanations met with opposition. Some suggested possible Egyptian, and even Buddhist, relationships. An argument for Gnosticism's origin as a Christian heresy was presented, but generally the Christian origin theses lost out—certainly the well-known one of nineteenth-century theologian Adolf Harnack who called Gnosticism "the acute Hellenization of Christianity." As the colloquium proceeded, increasing attention was given to Jewish influences.

Widengren hardly mentioned the Nag Hammadi discovery or its potential, but delegates were eager to hear the discussion following the second day's major paper by Martin Krause of Münster, West Germany. Between 1959 and 1961 Krause had spent considerable time cataloguing, transcribing, and photographing manuscripts in the Coptic Museum. He explained in detail at Messina what the professors already knew in general —that ten years after an international committee was formed to publish the Gnostic library (and twenty years after the discovery) the Gnostics were nearly as obscure as ever!

Only thirteen of the fifty-two tractates had reached print by then, and three of those were Nag Hammadi's duplicate copies of *The Apocryphon of John*. Less than 10 percent had appeared in English translation.

The frequently inexplicable roadblocks encountered between 1956 and 1966 disturbed many. "The slow publication of the collection has thus far been shrouded in a veil of mystery—not all of it engendered by the sometimes ponderous ways of scholarship," observed George MacRae, an American Jesuit who attended the Messina meeting.

Actually, the straits of scholarship in the preceding decade had Scylla-and-Charybdis-like characteristics. The French professors, key figures on the international committee, were snatched off the scholarship deck by the 1956 Suez Canal conflict. The committee never reconvened, apparently because of the break in Egyptian-French relations. In addition, museum director Labib was miffed when his name was omitted from a 1959 publication of *The Gospel of Thomas* produced by Puech, Quispel, Guillaumont, and others, according to the Frenchmen.

In this vacuum, scholars from Scandanavia and Germany were drawn down to Cairo and came up with arbitrary assignments from Labib. Frustrating to other researchers was that "channels through which the assignments . . . have been processed are not fully clear."

UNESCO had made an agreement with Egyptian officials in 1961 to form a new international translation committee but later decided to limit itself to publishing photographs of the pages. That alone promised to be of great help: Once photographs of the Nag Hammadi papyri were published, the manuscripts would be in the public domain and accessible to scholars who could read Coptic.

However, well after the U.N. agency's own deadline of March 1, 1965, only about 70 percent of the pages had been photographed. Picture-taking had been anything but meticulous in arrangement of fragments, and all blank pages were not being photographed. (Sometimes a blank page would bear blottings from the opposite page. If pieces of the page with script were missing, the blottings could at times produce the missing words.)

Charles-Henri Puech, Doresse's teacher, (left) and Dutch scholar Gilles Quispel (right) were at the Coptic Museum in the mid-1950's. Pahor Labib, successor to Mina as museum director, holds the magnifying glass.—Photo courtesy of Pahor Labib

"After some discussion (at Messina) . . ." MacRae wrote, "it was agreed that a committee should draft a report for presentation to UNESCO, urging that body to push forward its initial project by photographing the entire Nag Hammadi collection adequately and publishing photographs of all the works . . ."

The five-hundred-word cable began: "The Nag Hammadi codices are of quite fundamental significance for the study of Gnosticism, which is of itself of considerable importance for understanding the context of ideas out of which our modern world emerged." After detailing some of the problems, the appeal ended with the "fervent wish" of the assembled scholars that the project be completed "without delay." The cable was unanimously approved.

The three-man committee that prepared the cable consisted

of Martin Krause, whose speech sparked the discussion, Torgny Save-Soderbergh of Sweden, and an American New Testament theologian, James M. Robinson.

Robinson, then forty-one, was known in some theological circles for his book, *A New Quest for the Historical Jesus,* and other works, but he was a relative outsider at the Messina colloquium. He felt he had been named to the committee, a position which he would employ to shake loose dozens of previously inaccessible Nag Hammadi texts, for two reasons: "One, I could write a cable in English, which was the language they wanted, and two, in the discussions at the meeting, when anybody asked what was going on in Cairo—what had been photographed and the like—I had just come from Cairo and so I could say, 'Well, last week the UNESCO man there . . .' "

Robinson, a tall, lean, and intense professor from California, retained a Southern accent from his youth. He was graduating with honors from North Carolina's Davidson College and Columbia Theological Seminary about the time the Nag Hammadi manuscripts were being discovered.

Fascinated in the 1950s and early 1960s by even the limited amount of Nag Hammadi materials then available, Robinson began studying Coptic with some others while teaching at the School of Theology at Claremont (Calif.) and the Claremont Graduate School. He took a sabbatical leave in 1965–66 at the American School of Oriental Research in Jerusalem, Jordan, "to fill in blanks in my background on the manuscript and archeological side of New Testament studies." He spent part of his time in Jerusalem "plowing through" a translation of *The Apocalypse of Adam.* Later he explored the Nag Hammadi countryside.

Just weeks before the Messina conference, Robinson visited Cairo's Coptic Museum and asked to look at the original *Apocalypse* manuscript. "They were very nice, but they told me everything was under the control of UNESCO in Paris now," Robinson said. But the UNESCO official in Cairo disclaimed any U.N. authority over the manuscripts themselves. "In other words, I was getting the runaround," Robinson said.

Knowing that Krause had some pages photographed while he was in Cairo, Robinson went to the German Archeological Institute. The assistant director got out at least seventy sheets of photographs, and saying that he believed scholars should have access to such documents, loaned them to Robinson. "I spent three days and two nights in a dingy room in what used to be the Presbyterian mission in Cairo transcribing and proofreading the pages," recalled Robinson. "I got so that I could do about four pages an hour."

Following the Messina gathering, Robinson seized upon an offer by Krause to let the American copy his transcription of *The Letter of Peter to Philip* at Münster, West Germany. When Robinson arrived, he was informed that he was scheduled to lecture the next day. Caught unaware (a mailed request to Jerusalem missed him), Robinson was persuaded to speak by the offer to photocopy the Gnostic text transcription and allow him to prepare a lecture. Since Robinson had on hand a paper in German on Albert Schweitzer's *Quest of the Historical Jesus* that he could use for the lecture, he stayed up all night copying the rest of the notebook Krause had lent him—sixty pages from *Zostrianos*, the other Codex VIII treatise. Krause later gave Robinson page proofs to another tractate the German professor had translated and was readying for publication, *The Exegesis on the Soul*. "I was knocking myself out so I could come back to America with as many as one hundred fifty pages of otherwise inaccessible texts," Robinson said.

As early as July 1966, back in Southern California, Robinson told a *Los Angeles Times* interviewer that he hoped to translate, study, and eventually publish some of the material. Just how he had obtained the transcriptions "he does not care to reveal," said the *Times*.

Through a combination of tact, stealth, and persistence, Robinson soon would have a replica of practically the whole library.

He went to the Paris UNESCO office in 1967 in the role of secretary of the Messina ad hoc committee which had cabled the U.N. agency the year before. "I used that as an excuse to ask the man in charge there some questions," said Robinson. "Finally, he got tired of my asking him so many questions, and he said, 'You go through my file and *tell* me what I've got!' Thus, I got access to UNESCO photographs from 1967 more or less on, and in that way was able to copy out the whole library bit by bit."

Through grants from the National Endowment for the Humanities, Robinson launched English-language editions in a monograph series he edited together with Krause. Robinson channeled American scholarly activity on the library through the newly created Institute for Antiquity and Christianity within the Claremont Graduate School.

The first book from that project came out in 1975: *The Gospel of the Egyptians*, translated and analyzed by Frederik Wisse and Alexander Bohlig. Other books in the series were expected to follow quickly in succeeding years. While the English language project coedited by Robinson and Krause was the only complete series of its kind, the increased availability of the library has enabled other translations to appear singly or in limited collections.

Part of the impetus has come from the full publishing of manuscript pages and fragments in the series known as *The Facsimile Edition of the Nag Hammadi Codices*. Published by E. J. Brill of Leiden, Netherlands, the set of eleven volumes began appearing in 1972.

It wasn't until the winter of 1970–71 that plans were completed with UNESCO and Egyptian officials for publishing the facsimile edition. Robinson's efforts in the late 1960s and early 1970s, sandwiched between teaching duties, took him on several extended visits to Paris and Cairo to establish precise identification of page sequences and fragment locations.

At least two-thirds of the previous manuscript photography had to be redone because of poor arrangement of the fragments or because many pages were photographed with a dark background. When a letter only partially showed on the edge of a hole (or lacuna, as it is technically called), it was difficult to tell where the dark ink left off and the dark background began. White backgrounds were used for the new photos.

Assembling and studying the fragments was time-consuming, too, but it had its rewards. The title of one treatise, *Marsanes*, was found this way.

SIX

The Gnostic Redeemer Theory

James M. Robinson's fervent dedication to the Nag Hammadi Gnostic Library can be explained partly by his thoroughgoing nature, but vital keys lie in his experience with European scholarship. He completed his doctorate in contemporary theology under Karl Barth of Basel, Switzerland, but while working on his dissertation he spent the winter of 1950–51 in Marburg, West Germany. There he had a chance to hear some lectures and seminars by another theological giant of the era, Rudolf Bultmann, sixty-seven, who was to retire from teaching within months.

While teaching New Testament studies later at Emory University in Atlanta, Robinson avidly read volume after volume of Bultmann's works. "My swing from the Barthian camp into the Bultmannian took place actually after I had time to read it all," said Robinson.

A controversial figure for his "demythologizing" treatment of the New Testament, Bultmann characterized the descriptions of miraculous events, myths, and first-century world views presupposed by New Testament writers as natural for that period but inappropriate for modern man's understanding. Nevertheless, Bultmann declared that despite the ancient framework, the gospel message can still challenge modern individuals to new, liberating perspectives.

European and American scholars who sought to carry on the Bultmann tradition have generally become part of a "post-Bultmannian" wave which seeks to improve upon or augment the German master's research. Robinson more or less invented the term *post-Bultmannian.*

But, more than anything else, Bultmann's contention that Gnostic ideas were a major influence on the New Testament drove Robinson quite naturally to the Nag Hammadi studies. The discovery in Egypt offered "the golden opportunity to verify, update, revise as need be Bultmann's viewpoint on the religious context of the New Testament, which for him was primarily Gnostic," Robinson said in an interview.

Bultmann subscribed to many tenets of the "history of religions school" which tends to concentrate on the environment of a religion in its formative era and how it was shaped by history, rather than treating it simply as a supernatural occurrence. Many Christian critics of this school object to what they see as the tendency to regard Christianity as just one religion among others.

Bultmann saw Christianity as certainly shaping its own proclamation, but also as borrowing some concepts from the religious and philosophical thought of its day, intentionally or otherwise. Judaism provided a basic body of scripture, and the apocalyptic mood of some Jews in Jesus' day provided the idea of a messiah, resurrection of the dead, and coming divine judgment. The traditional Hellenistic culture called for a philosophical, rational approach to ideas and a Stoic detachment from the vicissitudes of life. The mystery cults spreading from Egypt, Syria, and Asia Minor also had some impact. The Christ was "conceived as a mystery deity, in whose death and Resurrection the faithful participate through the sacraments," Bultmann wrote in *Primitive Christianity in Its Contemporary Setting.*

Christianity asserts that humanity cannot redeem itself, that is, "save" itself from the world and the powers which hold sway in it. In this concept, primitive Christianity was greatly influenced by Gnostic ideas, said Bultmann. "Man's redemption," he wrote, "can only come from the divine world as an event," according to both the Gnostics and the Christians.

Most significantly, early Christians interpreted the person of

Jesus to a great extent in terms of the Gnostic redeemer myth, Bultmann contended. Jesus "is a divine figure sent down from the celestial world of light, the Son of the Most High coming forth from the Father, veiled in earthly form and inaugurating the redemption through his work." That picture of Jesus was dependent largely upon Gnostic imagery.

The Gnostic-redeemer-myth theory was not the invention of Rudolf Bultmann, but he outlined what became the classic model. Though most of the evidence he used was derived from the New Testament or later manuscripts, he considered the myth to predate Christianity's development.

As long ago as 1925, Bultmann proposed his version of the Gnostic redeemer myth and its significance for Christianity. As he summarized it years later, here are the major features of the myth which, he added, was probably told with many variations:

The Gnostic myth tells the fate of the soul, man's true inner self represented as "a spark of a heavenly figure of light, the original man." In primordial times, demonic powers of darkness conquer this figure of light, tearing him into shreds.

The sparks of light are used by the demons to "create a world out of the chaos of darkness as a counterpart of the world of light, of which they were jealous." The demons closely guarded the elements of light enclosed in humans. "The demons endeavor to stupefy them and make them drunk, sending them to sleep and making them forget their heavenly home." Some people nevertheless become conscious of their heavenly origin and of the alien nature of the world. They yearn for deliverance.

"The supreme deity takes pity on the imprisoned sparks of light, and sends down the heavenly figure of light, his Son, to redeem them. This Son arrays himself in the garment of the earthly body, lest the demons should recognize him. He invites his own to join him, awakens them from their sleep, reminds them of their heavenly home, and teaches them about the way to return."

The redeemer teaches them sacred and secret passwords, for the souls will have to pass the different spheres of the planets, watchposts of the demonic cosmic powers. "After accomplishing his work, he ascends and returns to heaven again to prepare a way for his own to follow him. This they will do when they die . . ."

The redeemer's work will be completed when he is able to reassemble all the sparks of light in heaven. That done, the world will come to an end, returning to its original chaos. "The darkness is left to itself, and that is the judgment."

Bultmann, who once suggested that the author of the Gospel of John was a convert from a Gnostic sect, also thought the Fourth Gospel reflected the Gnostic redeemer myth. The famous prologue to the Gospel is often cited in this regard:

> In the beginning was the Word, and the Word was with God, and the Word was God. He was in the beginning with God; all things were made through him, and without him was not anything made that was made. In him was life, and the life was the light of men. The light shines in the darkness, and the darkness has not overcome it (John 1:1–5).

The wording is vague and poetic enough to have invited innumerable interpretations in the history of Christianity. Taken together with John's later narration of Jesus' ministry and significance, the prologue pictures Jesus as "the preexistent Son of God, the Word who exists with him from all eternity," says Bultmann. He is sent by God as light for the world; indeed he *is* the light, the agent of revelation.

After accomplishing his Father's mission, Jesus returns to heaven to prepare the way for his own, that they may join him. Jesus says, "I am the way, and the truth, and the life; no one comes to the Father, but by me" (John 14:6) and, "Now is the judgment of this world, now shall the ruler of this world be cast out; and I, when I am lifted up from the earth, will draw all men to myself" (John 12:31–32).

According to Robinson, when Bultmann first worked out his theoretical model of the Gnostic redeemer myth, the German theologian referred to Proverbs 1:23–33 as the "most important passage . . . in which the whole myth is reflected."

In it, Wisdom raises her voice at the market and, from atop city walls, warns mortals to listen to her words. Many will ignore her "because they hated knowledge," and those who belatedly seek her will not find her. But those who heed her

*Rudolf Bultmann, the German theologian known for
"demythologizing" New Testament interpretation, also
developed a classic model of the Gnostic redeemer myth said
to have influenced early Christian descriptions of Jesus.*

words "will dwell secure and will be at ease, without dread of evil."

In other words, the personified Wisdom descends to the streets, markets, and city gates to offer "saving" knowledge to humanity, redemption from the fear of evil. Those who ignore her counsel will find it too late when they are beset with anguish and distress.

Wisdom is a savior of sorts in Proverbs 1, but in light of the Gnostic writings in the Nag Hammadi library it is important to notice that she is also a "laughing savior."

"How long will scoffers delight in their scoffing and fools hate knowledge?" asks Wisdom. For those who do, she says, "I . . . will laugh at your calamity; I will mock when panic strikes you . . ." She will mock those who mock her words.

Bultmann argued that echoes of the Gnostic redeemer myth can be seen in the New Testament. The Wisdom of Jewish literature and Gnostic myth becomes the personified "Word" in the prologue to the Gospel of John. He also saw a Gnostic myth behind Paul's allusion to a mysterious divine wisdom imparted only to mature believers (1 Cor. 2:6) and Paul's quoting of "a traditional hymn" which tells how Christ, a preexistent divine being, left the celestial world to take on human form, that of a servant (Phil. 2:6–11).

Bultmann intuitively looked to Jewish or Jewish-Christian baptismal sects as a possible source of Gnosticism, and in 1925 he wished for a clearer picture of the Essenes. The latter was remarkably provided by the Dead Sea Scrolls a quarter-century later, but as Bultmann entered retirement. Though the scrolls indicated steps toward Gnosticism, they did not contain a Gnostic redeemer, said Robinson.

But the prospect of finding a myth or myths of the Gnostic redeemer in the texts of the Nag Hammadi Gnostic Library stimulated and excited the American scholar whose Claremont office has one wall serving as a photographic gallery of noted theologians. Occupying the honored spot in the center is a picture of Rudolf Bultmann.

SEVEN

Return to the Cliffs

Although Robinson was drawn into Gnostic studies by the opportunity to prove, disprove, or improve Bultmann's theories of Gnostic influence on primitive Christianity, the American professor took little time out to do such a study in the first decade after the pivotal Messina colloquium. Conceivably, he could have prepared a definitive work on the subject since he personally had acquired access to either transcriptions or photographs of most of the library by the late 1960s. But Robinson was also determined to establish a model for team research, both for the series of English translations and for the publishing of manuscript photos. The thoroughness required has made these tasks time-consuming, and they were not completed when Robinson made another trip to Egypt in the fall of 1975.

The hazy circumstances of the discovery bothered Robinson. The story that the jar had been found buried in a stretch of barren land below the cliffs near Hamra Dom could not be verified. Could it have been discovered instead in one of the caves in the cliffs?

With the permission of Egyptian officials, Robinson made his third trip to the cliffs of Gebel et Tarif. He had been there in 1966 and 1974, but this time he returned with anthropologist Philip Hammond and two colleagues from the University of

James M. Robinson, New Testament theologian from Claremont, Calif., sits outside one of the caves in the side of Gebel et Tarif. The irrigated countryside near the Nile River is in the background.—Photo courtesy of P. Hedrick, Institute for Antiquity and Christianity

Utah. Hammond supervised the analysis of the ground which Doresse had been told was a Greco-Roman cemetery.

Magnetometer and resistivity tests of certain sections showed evidence of soil disturbance beneath the surface, but not that which would suggest a cemetery. Robinson also gave a sample of *sebakh*, the rich soil for which peasants were said to have been digging when they uncovered the jar, to a geologist for an opinion on its composition. The geologist said it was not soil enriched by human remains but topsoil that probably was left there periodically when the Nile overflowed its banks.

Most importantly, diligent inquiring by Robinson led him to a man who said he discovered the jar. Other sources corroborated that it was indeed Mohammed Ali El-Samman, a sixty-one-year-old camel driver still living in the area when Robinson interviewed him. "He said he was sifting for sebakh when he came across the jar," Robinson said. Robinson wonders whether sifting for the fine-grained soil is sometimes a euphemism for probing for archeological items.

El-Samman said it was the fall of 1945 when he broke the jar open, but details of the discovery and what followed were sketchy. Robinson's interview, done through an Arabic interpreter, was conducted while friends and family listened in, perhaps inhibiting El-Samman. The American first thought the camel driver identified a cave as the site. But El-Samman later indicated he found it near the talus, the sloping pile of sand and rocks at the base of the cliffs of Gebel et Tarif.

Amazingly finding the discoverer of the Gnostic treasure exactly thirty years after the fact—and nearly twenty-five years after Doresse seemed to learn as much as possible—has caused Robinson to ask whether the gaps in time make the new information untrustworthy. However, the accounts left by Doresse of his 1950 visit to the area were rather vague and never included the identity of the person or persons who actually found the jar. Like Robinson, Doresse was at the mercy of translators, but Doresse apparently failed to press for more precise information.

In the meantime, discoveries of another kind have been made in the manuscripts themselves. The sacred writings of the Gnostics, most of them never intended for the eyes of outsiders, were being studied by a growing circle of twentieth-century scholars.

The names of those who have advanced Gnostic studies are many. Prominent among them are George MacRae of Harvard Divinity School and Birger Pearson of the University of California, Santa Barbara—both editors in the Claremont-based Coptic Gnostic Library Project and both proponents of strong Jewish influence in the origins of Gnosticism.

THE JEWISH
CONNECTION

EIGHT

Dangerous Speculations

Early rabbis considered parts of the Bible too dangerous to discuss publicly or without mature guidance. Johanan ben Zakkai, a Jewish teacher prominent in the years after A.D. 70, passed along three time-honored warnings:

—The laws concerning incest should not be taught before as many as three people.

—The Genesis story of Creation should not be taught before two.

—The fantastic visions of God's throne-chariot in the Book of Ezekiel should not be taught before even one—unless that one is a knowledgeable sage himself.

It's better never to have lived, Zakkai continued, than to speculate over what is above, below, beyond, and in the opposite beyond. "And whosoever has no regard for the honor of his Creator," concluded Zakkai, "it were better for him had he not come into the world."

Could Johanan ben Zakkai have been thinking about the Gnostics with this advice? Gnostic heretics are not mentioned specifically in Jewish rabbinic literature, but some modern studies have shown "there were heretical Jewish Gnostics in Palestine, and they were referred to as 'minim,'" according to Birger Pearson. In some cases, the minim may have been Jewish Christians, but Pearson maintains the polemics in rabbinic writings make it clear that Jewish Gnostics, from the early second century on, if not earlier, "posed a great threat in many Jewish circles."

Zakkai's warning would apply in several ways to the Gnostics. They speculated about Genesis, and about what is above, below, and beyond, and ended up with a lack of regard for the Creator.

A certain amount of mysticism was tolerated by the Jewish sages in those days. Gershom Scholem, an authority on Jewish mysticism, contends that some precursors of the elaborate Kabbalah speculations of Medieval European Jews can be traced as far back as the first century B.C. in Palestine. Early Jewish mystics focused on the first chapters of Genesis and the opening chapter of Ezekiel.

Ezekiel begins with the prophet Ezekiel describing the heavens opening up. He saw visions of God, borne on a shining chariot whose four wheels were accompanied by four-faced living creatures. The Lord himself appeared to Ezekiel like a human form—half gleaming bronze, half fire—seated on a sapphirelike throne. Brightness was all about him.

It has been made obvious by key Nag Hammadi texts that early Gnostics developed an elaborate mythology in part from Genesis. Whether they engaged in a form of "throne mysticism" to the same extent is not clear.

The Jewish faith of the first centuries B.C. and A.D. was hardly the uniform religion described by later rabbis. "Prior to 70 A.D.," wrote D. S. Russell, "there was no recognized 'orthodoxy.' Nor was there any one party whose beliefs formed the norm by which Judaism could be judged."

Around 63 B.C. when the Roman Empire first exercised power over the Israelites, the authority to interpret Jewish law passed from the priestly aristocracy known as the Sadducees to the more liberal, popular Pharisees. The Sadducees preferred to keep the sacrificial cult activities centered at the Jerusalem Temple rather than allow ritual purity laws to be practiced in Jewish homes, as advocated by the Pharisees. The Roman destruction of the Temple in A.D. 70 eliminated the Sadducees' chief function.

Two other religious groups of that period were the Essenes and the Zealots. Seeking righteousness, many Essenes led severe lives. They believed in the immortality of the soul, were non-conformist regarding Temple rituals, and were thought to be pacifist, though the Qumran community of that sect as revealed by the Dead Sea Scrolls showed some military aspirations. The Zealots were known mainly for their unsuccessful revolt against the Romans in A.D. 6, involvement in the wider revolt of A.D. 66–70, and their last-ditch stand at Masada, which fell in A.D. 73.

Much of that picture of Jewish religious movements was provided by Josephus, a Jewish commander turned Roman historian. In his longest work, *Jewish Antiquities*, completed in A.D. 93, Josephus also mentioned the executions of Jesus, John the Baptist, and James, the brother of Jesus.

Yet another source of first-century religious life, of course, is the New Testament, which mentions not only the Pharisees and the Sadducees but also the "scribes"—jurists and teachers of the law.

The Pharisees apparently became more widely referred to as "rabbis" after A.D. 70, but it has been said that no one imagines that the day after the Temple's destruction someone like Johanan ben Zakkai woke up and said, "Today I am a rabbi." Historian Jacob Neusner suggests that the rabbinic tradition developed from the piety of the Pharisaic sect and the professional ideals of the scribes.

The heterodox aspect of Jewish religion before A.D. 70 also is demonstrated on the one hand by the Jewish Baptist sects, one of which was believed led by John the Baptist, and on the other hand by Philo of Alexandria, a Jew who sought to elucidate the rationality and philosophical insights inherent in the Jewish faith.

Religious literature of this period revealed another side of Judaism. Apocalyptic essays predicted cataclysmic events in which evil forces would be destroyed. It was "essentially a literature of the oppressed who saw no hope for the nation simply in terms of politics or on the plane of human history," wrote D. S. Russell.

The books which make up the Jewish Scriptures today were already composed, the last being Daniel, which was probably written about 165 B.C. Daniel has been called the first and greatest of the Jewish apocalyptic writings and was thought to have been prompted by the anti-Jewish religious measures of the Hellenized Syrian ruler, Antiochus IV Epiphanes. Two apocalyptic books in general circulation later—Jubilees and I Enoch—were held in honor by the Qumran Essenes, who had their own set of apocalyptic literature as well. Apocalyptic writers remained loyal to the God of Israel, though their inclusion of demons, angels, last-day prophecies, astrology, and cosmology showed the impact that the unsettled, religiously concerned Hellenistic age was having on the Jewish religion.

Hope for a miraculous intervention by God was expressed in typical apocalyptic books. "The expression of this belief is at times fanciful and exaggerated; but book after book throbs with the passionate conviction that all God had promised would surely come to pass," Russell said.

Logically, one might expect unfulfilled hopes would turn into bitter rejection for some believers. One scholar maintained for years that the destruction of the Jerusalem temple in A.D. 70 might have given birth to the Gnostic movement, but whether shattered Jewish apocalyptic hopes were transformed into Gnostic other-worldly yearnings will have to remain speculative at best.

Gilles Quispel of the Netherlands was among the first modern scholars of Gnosticism to propose a Jewish origin. As he put it, the characteristic features of Gnosticism "originated in Palestine among rebellious and heterodox Judaism," and Gnosticism proper was born "at the fringe of Judaism."

The anti-Jewish tenor of the Gnostic writings is so pronounced, however, says philosopher Hans Jonas, that more concrete evidence would have to be produced to prove that Jews turned against their own God so vehemently. Jonas authored a classic book on Gnosticism, *The Gnostic Religion*, based primarily on pre-Nag Hammadi resources. Disagreeing with some of Quispel's theses, Jonas said he would favor the origin of Gnosticism geographically close to the Jews with enough exposure to Judaism that the Jewish religion acted as a *catalyst*—but Jonas would not postulate an origin within Judaism. The spirit of Gnosticism, particularly as reflected in *The Apocryphon of John*, Jonas said, is one "of vilification, of parody and caricature, of conscious perversion of meaning, wholesale reversal of value signs, savage degrading of the sacred —of gleefully shocking blasphemy."

Nevertheless, in more recent years, some scholars working with the Nag Hammadi documents have become more convinced of a Jewish origin. Gnosticism must be conceived as an *internal* revolt against Judaism, maintains George MacRae, executive secretary of the Society of Biblical Literature.

The key to the Gnostic attitude, MacRae believes, is that the wisdom of the God of Israel was considered by Gnostics to be a disillusionment, even a deception. In addition, "the familiarity which Gnostic sources show toward details of Jewish thought is hardly one we could expect non-Jews to have."

There is still room in this theory for a foreign influence, he said, for without it the Jewish loss of confidence in the created world is unexplainable. "Whether of Orphic or Neo-Platonist or Iranian or other origin," MacRae said, "it must arise from the confrontation of religious and philosophical ideas in the syncretistic process. But whatever the precise origin of this anticosmicism, it is a foreign element that intrudes upon a form of Jewish thought and expression to drive it toward what we know as Gnosticism."

Pearson, writing about the Nag Hammadi codices in the *1974 Yearbook of the Encyclopedia Judaica,* said the texts contain "massive evidence concerning the Jewish elements in the development of Gnosticism." He cited primarily *The Apocalypse of Adam, On the Origin of the World, The Nature of the Archons, The Testimony of Truth,* and *The Apocryphon of John.* Pearson said that the Jewish traditions found in the Gnostic works were biblical and nonbiblical, "mainline" and "sectarian," and reflected both Palestinian and Egyptian-Jewish settings. "The Jewish element in Gnosticism must be seen as primary and not secondary."

Seeing merit in MacRae's theory of a religious revolt within Judaism, Pearson concludes in another paper, "As a result, a new religion—which can no longer be called 'Jewish'—is born."

Will that judgment stand up? Gershom Scholem, who described a milder type of Jewish Gnostic in his books, said the Nag Hammadi papyri give more support to the idea of a Jewish origin. At the same time, Scholem said in an interview that he believed the "commentaries on the Hebrew Bible are done by people whose connection with Judaism is doubtful . . . There are very curious misunderstandings, misreadings of the Bible."

A consensus among Nag Hammadi specialists on the origin of Gnosticism may be difficult to attain. Numerous scholarly papers have described the Gnostic use of Jewish lore, but there are indications that further research will place more emphasis on Gnostic familiarity with Egyptian and Greek thought.

It is tempting at this point, however, to envision Gnostic themes developing among Jews living in Palestine and/or Alexandria, groups of self-styled intellectuals intrigued with the mystical side of Greek philosophy and disillusioned with their own Jewish heritage.

NINE

The Envious God

The Nag Hammadi Gnostic Library would not be nearly as impressive as it is if the manuscripts had been written only decades before their late fourth-century placement in an earthen jar. The Gnostic tales are older, to be sure. Versions of the stories found near Nag Hammadi were occasionally reported by church fathers, notably Irenaeus of the late second century.

Crucial to Nag Hammadi studies is whether some myths and essays go back as far as the first century A.D., or even B.C. The earliest writings presumably would reveal the traces of Gnostic origins and whether they were pre-Christian. Judgments like these, often tentative, are made largely on how many parallels can be found with the style and content of religious compositions of those earlier periods.

A clumsily written text sometimes will cause more excitement among researchers than a lucid one. The latter often means the writer blended tradition and original thought into a coherent piece, making it tougher for analysts to dig down and uncover older ideas. Writings which only roughly make the transition from one section to another, however, tend to expose a distinct previous layer of thought.

Just such a treasure was found "buried" in the Nag Hammadi

treatise *The Testimony of Truth*, which is essentially a Christian Gnostic work.

Following a passage contrasting the virgin birth of Jesus with the natural birth of John the Baptist and an exhortation to seek after "mysteries," a horizontal line appears in the left hand margin of the papyrus page. The scribe was indicating a break in the text, but as Birger Pearson put it: "A source critic would see at this point—even without the scribe's mark—a clearly defined 'seam.' . . . We are encountering a literary source, previously existing and well-defined."

Inserted into *The Testimony of Truth* at this point was an older, rather primitive Gnostic piece of writing—a retelling of the Genesis story of the forbidden fruit plus some caustic comments on the Creator.

It is written in the Law concerning this, when God gave [a command] to Adam, "From every [tree] you may eat, [but] from the tree which is in the midst of Paradise do not eat, for on the day that you eat from it you will surely die."

But the serpent was wiser than all the animals that were in Paradise, and he persuaded Eve, saying, "On the day when you eat from the tree which is in the midst of Paradise the eyes of your heart will be opened."

And Eve obeyed, and she stretched forth her hand; she took from the tree; she ate; she also gave to her husband with her. And immediately they knew that they were naked, and they took some fig leaves (and) put on girdles.

But [God] came at the time of [evening] walking in the midst [of] Paradise. When Adam saw him he hid himself.

And he said, "Adam, where are you?"

He answered (and) said, "[I] have come to the fig tree."

And at that very moment God [knew] that he had eaten from the tree of which he had commanded him, "Do not eat of it." And he said to him, "Who is it who has instructed you?"

But Adam answered, "The woman whom you have given me."

And the woman said, "The serpent is the one who instructed me."

And he (God) cursed the serpent, and he called him "devil." And he said, "Behold, Adam has become like one of us, knowing evil and good." Then he said, "Let us cast him out of Paradise lest he take from the tree of life and eat and live for ever."

What sort is he, this God?

First, [he] envied Adam that he should eat from the tree of knowledge. And secondly he said, "Adam, where are you?" And God does not have foreknowledge; that is, since he did not know (it) from the beginning.

[And] afterwards he said, "Let us cast him [out] of this place, lest he eat of the tree of life and live for ever." Surely he has shown himself to be an envious slanderer.

And what kind of God is this? For great is the blindness of the commandments; and did they not reveal him? And he said, "I am the jealous God; I will bring the sins of the fathers upon the children until three (and) four generations" [see Exod. 20:5].

And he said, "I will make their heart thick, and I will cause their mind to become blind, that they might not know nor comprehend the things that are said" [see Isa. 6:10].

But these things he has said to those who believe in him [and] serve him!

The next passages mention other snakes in Scripture, including the episode of Moses' rod transforming into a snake and swallowing the serpents of magicians performing before the Pharaoh. Further on, *The Testimony of Truth* identifies the bronze serpent in Numbers 21:9 with Christ, indicating that the Christian nature of the tractate was resumed.

The style of the Adam and Eve story imbedded in the text, Pearson says, is typical of certain Jewish literature in the centuries around the beginning of the Christian era. Pearson termed this section in *Testimony* as a *midrash*, or commentary. In this case, the midrash was on the second and third chapters of Genesis.

The most cherished commentaries of the Jewish sages and early rabbis eventually were collected into works such as the Talmud, which was considered at times in Jewish history to be nearly as important as the Bible itself.

But the midrash in *The Testimony of Truth*, Pearson concludes, was written from a Gnostic point of view—an outraged Gnostic view at that!

Why, asked the writer, shouldn't Adam have eaten from the tree of knowledge? Wasn't this God angry because he was *envious* rather than because Adam disobeyed him?

There is not enough evidence to claim this commentator

was a sarcastic sage or a rebellious rabbi. But Pearson says the writer was familiar with not only Jewish Scriptures but also with the terminology and speculations of early rabbinic circles.

For instance, the Gnostic author describes the snake as "wiser" than any other wild creature—not "more subtle" as Genesis says. Yet *wise* was the adjective in keeping with Jewish commentary of the time: One early rabbinic source said the snake was "wise for evil." A saying attributed to one Rabbi Meir asserted that "the wisdom of the serpent was so great" that God had to inflict a penalty "proportionate to his wisdom"—cursed and condemned to crawl forever.

The Gnostic didn't resist the possible implication of God's question to Adam, "Where are you?" To the Gnostic it was evident that God, because of his "ignorance," didn't know where Adam was. Rabbis (and Christian leaders also) traditionally have explained that God's question actually was a reproach or a lament.

The midrash in *The Testimony of Truth* represents an early form of Gnostic thought, Pearson believes. "It is a gnostic midrash utilizing Jewish traditions. At the same time it is very simple and undeveloped, evidently a piece of 'primitive' Gnosticism." As to its date and place of composition, Pearson ventured a guess: the first century B.C. in Palestine or Syria.

TEN

The Wise Serpent

The Garden of Eden story is radically rewritten in three Nag Hammadi texts. The serpent tends to emerge heroically in the Gnostic rendition of Paradise, and the Creator God is portrayed as the ignorant ruler of a despicable world.

In one of these writings, *The Apocryphon of John,* the myriad of mythical details imbedded in a dialogue of Jesus with his disciples almost overwhelms the uninitiated reader. The two others, *The Nature of the Archons* and *On the Origin of the World,* are less complicated and have relatively few Christian touches.

An unprecedented look at Gnostic myth making is provided in all three works. Each displays parallels to Jewish commentary on the Bible typical of the period nearly two thousand years ago. But are they to be considered basically non-Christian?

The Nature of the Archons begins by saying that the "great apostle said to us concerning the powers of darkness: 'Our fight is not against flesh and blood, but it is against the powers of the world and what pertains to the spirit of wickedness.'" Paul is the unnamed "great apostle," and the loose quotation is from his Letter to the Ephesians (Eph. 6: 12).

But Roger Bullard has contended that Christian influence is discernible only in this introduction and in a section at the

End of "On the Origin of the World" and start of "The Exegesis on the Soul." (in Codex II) Title of the latter is offset in middle of page.

end of *The Nature of the Archons.* "This fact, plus the observation that these sections are detachable from a literary point of view, lead to the conclusion that Christian Gnostic touches have been added to a writing or writings that were not originally touched by Christian thought." There is no way of knowing from the document itself if the stories are pre-Christian, he added, but there is nothing to preclude it either.

In some ways, *The Nature of the Archons* takes off where *The Testimony of Truth* midrash ended. The primitive and caustic commentary in *Testimony* characterized the Hebrew God in terms of blindness, ignorance, and arrogance but still called him respectfully "God."

Archon was a word used commonly by Gnostics for the Hebrew God, a word meaning "ruler" in Greek, the lingua franca of the Hellenistic age in East Mediterranean lands. The Creator God was sometimes called the "First Archon" or the "Great Archon" by Gnostics to distinguish him from his malicious associates, also called "archons," "powers," or "authorities."

Gnostics, studying Genesis for the story behind the story, could hardly miss the use of the first person plural—"Let us make man in our image, after our likeness . . ." "Behold, the man has become like one of us, knowing good and evil . . ." The deity which expelled mankind from Paradise was seen as an evil collective force—Archons, the arch-enemies of humanity.

The quotation from Paul conveniently fit the Gnostic picture of the battle against the cosmic powers, though Paul would not have included his God in that number. *The Nature of the Archons,* in what is probably its original opening, says bitterly that of all the cosmic powers, "their great one is blind." Because of his might, ignorance, and arrogance, he declared he was God and that there was no one beside him. But when his boast was heard in the higher realms, a voice came forth: "You are wrong, Samael." Samael is quickly defined as meaning "the god of the blind," and, the text adds, "his thoughts were blind."

When the chief Archon brags another time in *Archons,* he is reproached again from above by a voice calling him "Saclas."

The manuscript says without elaboration that Saclas is interpreted "Ialdabaoth."

It is not clear from *Archons* whether all three names were applied interchangeably by some Gnostics to the Creator God. The Nag Hammadi discovery, fortunately, supplied scholars with dozens of texts for comparison. (Indeed, the very bulk of the cache forced many scholars with limited access to the manuscripts to make only tentative or narrow statements about the Gnostic writings lest the unpublished tractates turn up something to contradict their views.)

The same epithets for God did occur in other Nag Hammadi books. The longer versions of *The Apocryphon of John* say simply, and with derision, "This weak Archon, therefore, had three names. The first name is Ialdabaoth. The second is Saclas. The third is Samael."

The names are thought to derive from Aramaic, a language spoken in Palestine and Syria, similar to Hebrew, and said by many to have been the language of Jesus. Samael in Jewish lore is often the angel of death, but in Aramaic it means the "blind god." Saclas means "fool" in Aramaic. Ialdabaoth is said by some scholars to mean "child of chaos," an etymology strengthened by the Gnostic myth in the library which tells of Ialdabaoth's birth from the depths of Chaos.

The Gnostic myth starts in the highest realms. *The Nature of the Archons* described it this way in Bullard's translation:

> Above, in the infinite aeons, is Imperishability. Sophia, she who is called Pistis, wanted to make a work by herself, without her partner. And her work became the images of heaven. There is a curtain between those above and the aeons which are beneath.

Sophia is the feminine Greek word for "wisdom," but here she is a personified deity. Sophia is sometimes called Pistis, the feminine Greek word for "faith," and sometimes Pistis Sophia, but scholarship has shown Sophia to be the name central to the Gnostic myth. The aeons, or "ages," were considered particularly ominous, fateful realms in the philosophical views of those days.

The curtain, or veil, between the aeons above and beneath

caused a problem, leading to the creation of Ialdabaoth/Sac-las/Samael:

> And a shadow came into being beneath the curtain, and that shadow became matter. And that shadow was cast forth successively, and the form became a work in the matter like an abortion. It took shape from the shadow. It became an arrogant beast in the form of a lion. It was androgynous . . .

Thus did the great Archon come into being.

The same story is told more elaborately and lucidly in *On the Origin of the World*. Pistis Sophia is disturbed by her deficiency—she tried to create by herself a work "like the light which first came to be" and created only a series of formless things which the text compares to a woman's afterbirth. Sophia turns to the Abyss, breathes mightily, and out of the waters appears an archon ". . . lion-like [and] androgynous, with a great authority within himself, but not knowing whence he came."

The story continues roughly the same in *The Nature of the Archons* and *On the Origin of the World*. After Sophia had created the archon out of the watery, chaotic abyss, she withdrew to her light and caused him to form the heavens and the earth.

The creation of man involved more than one Adam, according to *Origin*. The first was a "Light-Adam" who passed through all the seven heavens of the earth, and another was the human Adam shaped by the archons from the dust of the earth.

Thinking himself the supreme Lord, Ialdabaoth recklessly declared, "If someone exists before me, let him appear in order that we might see his light."

Immediately, the Light-Adam appeared with a wondrous "human likeness." Just as quickly, he withdrew, but not before he was seen by the "authorities," the minion-archons of the great Archon, Ialdabaoth. They laughed at their boastful chief who was shown up by the Light-Adam's appearance.

Stung by the laughter, the Archon suggested a plan to make the Light-Adam subservient to them:

> . . . let us create a man from the earth according to the image of our body and according to the likeness of that [one], and

let him serve us in order that when that one [the Light-Adam] sees his likeness and loves it, he will no longer destroy our work, but those who are begotten by the light we will make serve us through all the time of the aeon.

The "two Adams" story is not as wild as it sounds. The Bible gives two versions of the creation of Adam (Gen. 1:27 and 2:7), and the Jewish philosopher Philo of Alexandria, a contemporary of Jesus, said that the first Adam was a heavenly model for the second.

After the human Adam is formed, God or Sophia breathes into his face, depending on whether the story is told by *Archons* or *Origin*. Adam moves about but is unable to rise, an idea consistent with some Jewish speculation around the first century A.D. Then, says *Origin:*

Sophia sent Zoe, her daughter, who is called "Eve," as an instructor in order that she might raise up Adam, in whom there is no psyche [soul] so that those whom he would beget might become vessels of the light. When Eve saw her companion-likeness cast down she pitied him, and she said, "Adam, live! Rise up upon the earth!"

Immediately, her words became a work for when Adam rose up, immediately he opened his eyes. When he saw her, he said, "You will be called 'mother of the living' because you are the one who gave life to me."

What happened to Adam's rib? *Archons* makes no mention of it. *Origin* says that the rib story was a falsehood perpetrated by the archons, who counseled each other: "Let us teach him in his sleep as though she came to be from his rib so that the woman will serve and he will be lord over her." The Gnostics, by contrast, claimed man was indebted to woman for bringing him to life!

Discrediting the rib story on other grounds would not be unheard of from a Jew of that period. Philo of Alexandria, who was not a Gnostic, said the Genesis story about Eve coming from the rib of a man was "myth." Philo asked rhetorically, "For how could anyone concede that a woman or any person at all came into being out of man's side?"

The Gnostic *Apocryphon of John* is more blunt—"And not

as Moses said, 'his rib.' " (Moses was traditionally thought to have written down the first five books of the Bible.)

The prohibition against eating from the tree of knowledge is repeated in *Archons* and *Origin*. The stage is set for the serpent. In *Archons*, Sophia apparently enters the serpent, who thereby acquires the title of Instructor. *Origin*, on the other hand, says that Sophia created the Instructor to teach Adam and Eve the truth about their origins. Sophia is ironically the creator, or mother, of both the snake-Instructor and Eve, according to *Origin*.

> Then the one who is wiser than all of them, one who was called "the wild beast," came. And when he saw the likeness of their mother, Eve, he said to her: "What is it that god said to you?—'Do not eat from the tree of knowledge'?
>
> She said: "He said not only 'Do not eat from it' but 'Do not touch it, lest you die.' "
>
> He said to her, "Don't be afraid. You will surely not [die], for [he knows] that when you eat from it your mind will be sobered and you will become like the gods, knowing the distinctions which exist between the human evil and the good. For he said this to you, being jealous lest you eat from it."
>
> Then Eve was confident of the words of the Instructor, and she peered into the tree . . .

She ate the fruit of the tree and gave of it to her husband to eat also. Their minds were opened, continues *Origin*. When the archons questioned Adam and Eve and learned what the serpent had done, they approached the serpent-Instructor, but their "eyes were blinded by him."

Powerless to do anything to the serpent, the archons merely cursed him and then cursed Eve.

> After the woman they cursed Adam and the earth because of him and the fruit. And everything which they created they cursed. There is no blessing from them. It is impossible that good be produced from evil.

The above lines sum up well the Gnostic attitude toward the cursed world and the denial of godlike knowledge to mankind.

But the storytelling was unrelenting in its ridicule. *Origin* said the archons were furious particularly because Adam and Eve saw for the first time that the archons had the faces of animals, and the first couple "loathed" them. (Ialdabaoth, of course, had the appearance of a lion, and *The Apocryphon of John* says some of the archon's fellow powers bore the faces of an ape, a hyena, a dragon, and a donkey.)

The archons called the Instructor "a wild beast," but a Gnostic reader would say this was like the pot calling the kettle black. Not only that, says *Origin*, "The interpretation of the 'wild beast' is 'the instructor.'" The two words have the same linguistic root in Aramaic; so what *Origin* was saying was that the opponents were unaware that their attempted slander was a compliment.

Another significant play on words in Aramaic involved the similarity of the words for "Eve," "serpent," and "instruct." The snake contains the Instructor in *Origin* and *Archons*. And in *The Testimony of Truth* midrash the verb is pointedly used —the serpent "instructed" Eve and Eve "instructed" Adam. Rabbinical literature preserved a similar double entendre with a Rabbi Aha speaking, as if addressing Eve: "The serpent was thy serpent, and thou art Adam's serpent."

Pearson indicates that because the wordplays would have been most effective in Aramaic, a Palestinian or Syrian locale is suggested for the origin of these myths-interpretations.

Somehow disillusioned by the Jewish faith, the Gnostic outrage in the excerpt from *The Testimony of Truth* becomes bitter irony or sarcasm in *The Nature of the Archons* and *On the Origin of the World*.

The Gnostic writers mock the Creator—Yahweh, the God of Israel—turning to the language of the ordinary people, Aramaic, for sarcastic wordplays and crude names. For their principal heroine-deities (Sophia, Pistis, Zoe) they often drew from the language of culture and philosophy, Greek.

ELEVEN

The "Rape" of Eve; Norea the Ark Burner

Gnostic myth making, in some circles, regarded Eve and the wife of Noah as brave foremothers of the Gnostic elect. Inasmuch as they were considered to be the daughter and granddaughter of Sophia, they were able to stand up to the evil archons better than their husbands.

The great Archon's underlings were enthralled when they first saw the lovely Eve talking with Adam in Paradise. She had a certain radiance about her.

"Now, come!" decided the descendants of darkness in *On the Origin of the World*. "Let us seize her and let us cast our seed on her," they plotted, "so that if she is polluted, she will not be able to go up to her light, but those whom she will produce will serve us."

They chased her, but it was fruitless.

"Eve, being a power, laughed at their purpose," says *Origin*. She darkened their eyes and left her likeness beside Adam. She fled into the tree of knowledge, but to her pursuers it looked as if she entered and *became* the tree. The archons scattered in fear.

Later, returning to the sleeping Adam, the archons saw what they thought was Eve lying beside her mate. They villanously "cast their seed upon her." The heaven-sent Eve had tricked them, of course.

The Nature of the Archons has a similar rape story, but, like the Bible, has the real Eve giving birth by Adam to Cain and Abel.

On the Origin of the World, however, says that Eve's counterfeit image bears her children by the archons. This was done, explains the text, so that resultant generations would contain the seeds of light dispersed earlier in the matter that makes up the world. Unknown to the evil rulers of the world, their offspring would become "a hedge for the light," an expression used twice in *Origin.*

A "hedge for the light" apparently means about the same as a famous instruction the earliest rabbis said was passed down from Moses—"make a hedge for the Torah." To Jewish students of the Torah (the first five books of the Bible) this meant "to keep the divine revelation from harm so that the sacred enclosure, so to speak, might always be free and open for the human to contemplate the divine," wrote R. Travers Herford.

In the Gnostic scheme, mankind is the hedge, not for the biblical revelations, but for the scattered particles of divine light loosed when Sophia created the Creator God.

U.S. scholar Orval Wintermute says the stance in *Origin* goes beyond simple commentary on Genesis to a theological position. Man has a nature inherited from both the worldly archons and the highest light. "The primary task of man in the world is to repudiate the archons," said Wintermute. Man needs power from above to do it, but being a half-breed, he is also "the agent of a peculiar justice" by denouncing his makers, the archons.

The idea of heavenly powers mating with humans was not derived by Gnostic authors from non-Jewish mythology. The sixth chapter of Genesis begins by saying "the sons of God," which scholars say refers to angels, taking as their wives the fair daughters of men. The children born to them "were the mighty men . . . of old, the men of renown." However, the Bible continues, men became wicked, and God was sorry he made them. He saw favor in Noah only.

True to the Gnostic reverse interpretations, *The Nature of the Archons* claims that men were getting better. The archons decided to wipe out the humans with a flood, except for Noah and his children and the birds and the animals. Noah was told to build an ark and place it atop Mt. Seir. This place name does not occur in Genesis, but it does in one of the psalms which refers to the great deluge.

The wife of Noah was unnamed in Genesis but was called Norea by the Gnostics. She was also the virgin daughter of Eve, according to *Archons*.

Noah bars Norea from entering the ark; so she blows against the craft and burns it down. Noah builds another ship, but before his wife has a chance to destroy the second ark, the archons confront her.

"Your mother Eve came to us," said the chief Archon in a translation by Bentley Layton.

"It is you who are the Rulers of Darkness; you are accursed. And you did not know my mother," responded Norea. "Instead it was your female counterpart that you knew. For I am not your descendant." (*Archons* had indicated Eve had her children by Adam.)

The Archon's face turns black, and he demands of her: "You must render service to us, [as did] also your mother Eve . . ."

Norea cries for help from the highest God, and a golden angel clothed in snowy white descends from heaven, causing the archons to withdraw.

"Who are you?" asked Norea.

"It is I who am Eleleth, Sagacity, the Great Angel who stands in the presence of the Holy Spirit. I have been sent to speak with you and save you from the grasp of the Lawless. And I shall teach you about your Root," said the angel.

Eleleth, identified in *The Apocryphon of John* as one of four heavenly illuminators, tells Norea the story of how the world and the archons came into being after Sophia tried to procreate without a partner. The angel assures Norea that she and her children will be safe from the powers because her soul came from the Imperishable Light.

The Apocryphon of John talks about the deluge but not about Norea. Noah is the Gnostic hero in this case. He and the men of the "unwavering [Gnostic] generation" are saved from Ialdabaoth's flood when they are hidden in a light-cloud while the earth is covered by "darkness" (the watery deep). The *Apocryphon* typically contradicts Genesis: "Not as Moses said, 'They were hidden in an ark.'"

Norea is featured in another Nag Hammadi tractate, *The Thought of Norea*. In one sequence she cries out for help from above, and "four holy helpers" intercede for her on behalf of the Father.

Many versions of the Norea story must have existed. The author of *Origin* refers his readers to several other books for details on the various heavens and powers to which he alludes. Two texts he cited were "the first book of Noraia" and "the first treatise of Oraia." Obviously, the heroine's name was variously spelled. Even *Archons* alternated between spelling it Norea and Orea.

According to Epiphanius, one group of Gnostics fabricated a book called *Noria*. The church father said these heretics claimed Noria, Noah's wife, was barred from entering the ark, so she burned it—not once, but *three* times.

Epiphanius said the Gnostics named Noah's wife Noria in an attempt to translate Pyrrha ("Fiery"), the flood heroine of Greek mythology, into an Aramaic name suggesting "fire." (They were wrong, said Epiphanius, who claimed her real name was Barthenos.) Bullard suggested Orea is the basic name, originating from a fire-breathing snake of Egyptian mythology, the uraeus.

Increased study of the Nag Hammadi library has demonstrated that the most fruitful place to look for such explanations is in Jewish speculation. The rabbis said Noah's wife was named Naamah and was a descendant of Cain. She bore a tradition of seductive wickedness in Jewish speculative circles. Naamah means "pleasing, lovely" in Hebrew. Pearson suggests that the Gnostics translated Naamah into the Greek for "pleasant, lovely," which is Horaia, and that Horaia came also to be spelled Orea and Norea.

For all of Norea's fiery charms, it is still Sophia who remains the most desirable heroine in primitive Gnosticism. She is Wisdom, after all, sought by those in pursuit of "gnosis."

For the origins of the Gnostic Sophia, scholars have looked to Judaism. Her literary lineage stems from the so-called biblical wisdom literature in which Wisdom becomes personified.

(Two feminine gender nouns for "Wisdom" were used—either the Hebrew "Hokhmah," as in the Old Testament's Proverbs, or "Sophia," the Greek equivalent used in the Jewish apocrypha such as the Wisdom of Solomon and Sirach.)

"Wisdom is radiant and unfading, and she is easily discerned by those who love her, and is found by those who seek her" (Wisd. of Sol. 6:12).

She also is pictured as a heavenly power existing from the beginning of time. "The Lord created me at the beginning of his work, the first of his acts of old," she says in Proverbs 8.

"I dwelt in high places, and my throne was in a pillar of cloud," she declares in Sirach 24:4. "Alone I have made the circuit of the vault of heaven and have walked in the depths of the abyss."

A wealth of imagery fed the speculative mind of the Gnostic. George MacRae identifies numerous parallels in comparing Wisdom in Jewish literature and Sophia in Gnostic writings. Besides the common heavenly abode, says MacRae, both were identified with a Spirit, were instrumental in the creation of the world, strengthened Adam, communicated wisdom and revelations to men, and descended into the world of humanity.

The Gnostic Sophia reascends to the light in texts such as *The Nature of the Archons* and *On the Origin of the World*. That theme is generally absent in Jewish works because of the desire to show that Wisdom finds her home in Israel.

"Cumulatively," said MacRae, "this long list of parallels between the Jewish Wisdom and the Gnostic Sophia makes it virtually impossible to rule out all influence of the former on the latter, and makes it at least probable that some kind of (no doubt perverse) use of the Jewish Wisdom figure lies at the source of the Gnostic myth."

Sometimes a single passage in the Jewish wisdom literature seems to have prompted several Gnostic ideas. An example is the Wisdom of Solomon 7:25: "For she [Wisdom] is a breath of the power of God, and a pure emanation of the glory of the Almighty; therefore nothing defiled gains entrance into her."

The lustful archons attempted to "defile" the daughter of Sophia (Eve) but were tricked into raping her substitute image. Likewise, they were unsuccessful with the virgin granddaughter of Sophia (Norea).

George MacRae, one of the editors of the English language project to publish the full library, studies papyrus fragments from the inside of a leather cover in the Nag Hammadi library. Receipts and other scraps were used to stiffen the covers; they have yielded dates from A.D. 333 to 348.—Los Angeles Times photo, Steve Fontanini

As "a breath of the power of God," the Gnostic Sophia in *Origin* breathes life into a shapeless mass to form Ialdabaoth, and she breathes life into Adam.

The Gnostic Sophia is linked with the highest God and thus could be considered a "pure emanation" of this God. But in other, apparently later, treatises a Gnostic ambivalence toward Sophia becomes apparent. The problem was that the Gnostic Sophia, a close associate of the highest God, gave birth to the evil Creator God and the debilitating world. Early Gnostic myth makers were undoubtedly asked: How could a "pure emanation" of the highest God be responsible for all this evil?

The Gnostics evidently tried to resolve this by dividing the female deity into a pure version and a fallen version. Various Gnostic groups explained the division differently.

In *The Apocryphon of John* a deity named Barbelo stands next to the Father, and Sophia operates on a lower level. The theology of the Gnostic Valentinus contained a higher and a lower Sophia, according to church father Irenaeus. *The First Apocalypse of James* indicates that the "imperishable gnosis" is Sophia who is with the Father, but there is also Achamoth (a variant spelling of the Hebrew word for "wisdom") who is an inadequate Sophia. *The Gospel of Philip* says there are two Sophia figures: Echamoth, who is simply Sophia, and Echmoth, who is the Sophia of death.

The process seems clear, says MacRae. God's Wisdom is first personified in Gnostic writings, "then split, lest God's transcendence be compromised."

Sophia-like figures in some other Gnostic stories are not split but are errant in their ways—such as the "thought" of God in Simon Magus' system who was finally rescued while imprisoned in the body of a whore. Sophia is not mentioned by name in *The Gospel of Truth*, but her myth seems to underlie the vague force named Error, which is involved in a fall and creates the world of matter.

How does the *descent* of Wisdom in Jewish literature become the *fall* of Sophia in Gnosticism? MacRae suggests the principal source is the error of Eve in the Garden of Eden.

"Jewish tradition from biblical times onward had a keen sense of the disorder in the world resulting from the fall of the first couple . . ." MacRae said. "Now the Gnostic, who began with a more radical notion that the world itself was disorder, would seek to explain this situation by postulating a fall in the (divine regions) of which the fall of man is but an inferior copy."

Although Jewish and Christian theology usually put the ultimate blame on Adam for the fall, a plain reading of Genesis shows that the woman took the fruit, wanting to become wise, or as the serpent put it, to be "like God, knowing good and evil." This was Sophia's trouble, too, the Gnostics said, because she wanted to give birth to something without a partner or to comprehend God—feats possible only by God himself.

"One would miss an essential insight into the Gnostic myths if he failed to realize that a close correspondence is intended there between the celestial world . . . and the material world of men," said MacRae. The Gnostic tales—often occult, sometimes inept—projected the events and characters of Genesis onto a higher plane to offer humanity an altogether different view of life's meaning.

TWELVE

The Descendants
of Seth

Practically anyone today could tell you that Adam and Eve had two sons, Cain and Abel. Could they name a third son? This child, Seth, was provided by God as a replacement for the slain Abel, according to Genesis, and was not born until Adam was 130 years old.

Jewish speculation about Adam and Seth was common in the first centuries. Adam had abstained from sexual intercourse all during the years before Seth's birth, some commentaries said. But in that time succubi often visited Adam as he slept, causing involuntary emissions of semen, and incubi debauched the sleeping Eve, with demon offspring resulting from both sexual deceptions. Other "details" about the lives of the Bible's first couple were known before the Nag Hammadi discovery from *The Life of Adam and Eve,* a non-Gnostic text believed by some to have been written before A.D. 70.

While Sophia and other heroines were considered important mythical forerunners of the Gnostics, it is apparent that many Gnostics believed themselves the spiritual descendants of Seth. That is quite understandable. Josephus said legend had it that Seth was a virtuous man, leaving generations who imitated his ways and lived happy, prosperous lives.

These descendants were the discoverers of astrology, said Josephus. That discovery and others were inscribed on two pillars, one of brick and the other of stone, in hopes of preserving them for posterity. According to Josephus, Adam had predicted that great devastation lay ahead, once by violent fire and again by a mighty flood.

Nag Hammadi has added to the Adam-Seth tales some previously unknown texts, but containing the usual Gnostic twists. The most important may be *The Apocalypse of Adam*, which purports to be the words of the dying Adam to Seth. Some legends reported by Josephus are seen in the *Apocalypse*. It is written in the "last testament" literary style used both in the Bible and in turn-of-the-era, biblical-style books. As such, some scholars consider it one of the oldest texts in the Nag Hammadi collection. It begins:

> The revelation which Adam taught his son Seth in the seven hundredth year, saying:
> "Listen to my words, my son Seth. When God created me out of the earth along with Eve your mother, I went about with her in a glory which she had seen in the aeon from which we had come forth. She taught me a word of knowledge of the eternal God. And we resembled the great eternal angels, for we were higher than the God who had created us . . ."

The Creator God, however, vented his wrath on Adam and Eve, causing their glory and knowledge to leave them. "And we served him in fear and slavery," Adam said. It was then that Adam began to feel a sweet desire for Eve, and he began to be more conscious of his mortality.

Because of that, Adam said he wanted to pass on what knowledge he could to Seth and his progeny.

Adam predicted that the wrathful Creator God would seek to destroy Seth's seed, the men of "gnosis," with a flood. Noah and his household would be saved to repopulate the earth and serve the evil deity, but angels would rescue the Gnostics by taking them aloft. After the flood, the subservient Noah would advise his sons Ham, Japheth, and Shem to serve God "in fear and slavery all the days of your life."

The Gnostics would return to earth to be joined by a specific number of Ham's and Japheth's descendants. "Four hundred thousand men will come and enter into another land and sojourn among those who have come from the great eternal knowledge," Adam prophesied. Most descendants of Ham and Japheth who remained loyal to the Creator would complain to their God (called Sakla here) that the four hundred thousand were living in glory despite their defection.

Fire, sulphur, and asphalt would be cast down on the Gnostics—allusions to punishment meted out to the biblical Sodom and Gomorrah. (The Gnostic reversal at work again: Sodom and Gomorrah were really inhabited by the righteous.) The angels Abrasax, Sablo, and Gamaliel would descend to save them from the fire, however, by taking them above the domain of the evil powers.

The third and final era would be launched by the coming of the Illuminator ("Phoster") of knowledge, whose significance will be discussed later.

The Apocalypse of Adam closes with a prediction that these words will be inscribed on a rock on a high mountain. The text concludes:

> This is the hidden knowledge of Adam which he gave to Seth, which is the holy baptism of those who know the eternal knowledge through those born-of-the-word and the imperishable Illuminator, who came from the holy seed: Jesseus, Mazareus, Jessedekeus.

Several scholars believe *The Apocalypse of Adam* arose out of a non-Christian, Jewish milieu. They call attention to the parallels to the Adam-Seth literature of the first century A.D. and to the dying-words framework of The Testament of the Twelve Patriarchs, a Jewish apocryphal work.

The first professor to publish a translation of the *Apocalypse*, Alexander Bohlig of Germany, contended it was a product of pre-Christian Gnosticism though he admitted that the three names at the very end might be a distorted utterance of Jesus of Nazareth. The fact that Jesseus, Mazareus, Jessedekeus are at the document's conclusion makes it likely that Christian influence, if it was that, only affected the text slightly and after the bulk of the narrative was written.

The three names appear twice in *The Gospel of the Egyptians*, a manuscript evidently related to the *Apocalypse* but written in a later period. Jesus appears in *The Gospel of the Egyptians*, though he is only a part of the story, not the cen-

tral character. The dominant role is played by the "great Seth."
Seth passes through three crises common to several Gnostic
writings—flood, fire, and the judgment of the archons.

The Gospel of the Egyptians was one of the first Nag Hammadi manuscripts examined by Jean Doresse, and it particularly
fascinated him. Doresse's study of the papyrus texts, often
relatively cursory, led him to suggest that the bulk of the
library was Sethian, that is, written by Gnostics who considered themselves inheritors of "the seed of Seth." Doresse
was aware of Valentinian Christian Gnostic writings, Hermetic
(Greco-Egyptian) texts, and other works in the Nag Hammadi
library, but further study has shown that the diversity was
greater than Doresse was willing to concede.

References to Seth in a Nag Hammadi text do not necessarily mean it is a Sethian composition, says Frederik Wisse.
"There were Sethians—Gnostics who identified themselves as
members of the race of Seth. They used this designation to
indicate their heavenly origin and their basic dissimilarity from
the rest of mankind." But "it is evident that different myths
became associated with the appellation 'race of Seth.' "

Which myths originated with the Sethians is difficult to say.
The Gnostics generally seemed to care little about establishing
creeds or standardized myths. Each composition is highly in-
dividualistic though some themes and names reappear in several
texts.

A Nag Hammadi treatise such as *The Three Steles of Seth*
is an example. It claims to be a revelation by a Dositheos about
the inscriptions of Seth, "the father of the living and immov-
able race," on three stone steles.

On the first stele Seth praises Adam, his father. (However,
it seems the praise here is directed to the heavenly Adam, who
is similar to the Light-Adam pictured in *On the Origin of the
World.*)

The second stele is addressed to the first of the aeons, the
"male virgin [sic] Barbelo, the first glory of the invisible Father, she who is called 'perfect.' " Perhaps reflecting the androgynous nature of Barbelo, Seth refers to Barbelo as thou,
feminine gender, most of the time, but also uses the masculine
form of thou. Barbelo, or Barbelon, appears in several other

Gnostic texts, including *The Apocryphon of John, The Gospel of the Egyptians, Zostrianos, Melchizedek,* and *Marsanes.*

Seth's third stele rejoices over the sight of the preexistent, unnameable Spirit. ("We have seen thee with the mind.") The purpose of this glorification and praise was then revealed: "As we are capable, we bless thee, for we were saved every time when we glorified thee. Therefore we should glorify thee so that we may escape safely to eternal salvation."

The Three Steles of Seth makes no distinction between a higher God and an ignorant Creator God, dualism usually considered indispensable for a text to be called Gnostic, said James M. Robinson. The California scholar would place it into a group of philosophic Gnostic treatises with affinities to neo-Platonism, but he notes that the prominence of the heavenly Adam and Barbelo points to a close relationship with Jewish Gnosticism. Significantly, nothing indicates Christian influence, and "Jewish tradition is presupposed but had receded into the background."

Jewish tradition of nearly two thousand years ago is said to be more represented, of course, in Nag Hammadi texts such as *The Apocalypse of Adam, The Apocryphon of John, On the Origin of the World, The Nature of the Archons,* and the excerpt from *Testimony of Truth.* If Pearson and MacRae are correct, the myths these texts contain may date from that period and represent the beginnings of the Gnostic religion. Whether arising as a revolt within Judaism or as a movement on the fringes, the movement is no longer essentially Jewish but Gnostic.

The same thing can be said to some extent about the beginnings of the Christian religion in the first century—the faith in the man-God was a departure from Judaism; it was no longer essentially Jewish but Christian.

The inevitable happened. Some believers became both Christian and Gnostic. From the perspective of the twentieth century the two may seem incompatible, but both new religions (perhaps both Judaic offshoots) would have been in a state of flux in their early stages. Both presumably were a disliked minority in Jewish areas. At any rate, the writings of Christian Gnostics make up a major portion of the Nag Hammadi library.

WILL THE
REAL SAVIOR
PLEASE
STAND UP?

THIRTEEN

The Historical Jesus

"I won't say the papers misquote me," said Sen. Barry Goldwater at one point in his unsuccessful 1964 campaign for the U.S. presidency, "but I sometimes wonder where Christianity would be today if some of those reporters had been Matthew, Mark, Luke, and John." Columnist Walter Lippmann's response a few days later was that "the senator might remember that the evangelists had a more inspiring subject."

That exchange is pertinent here not so much for what it says about journalism as for illustrating a common misconception about the Christian Gospels. The so-called synoptic Gospels of Matthew, Mark, and Luke were written to a great extent in a matter-of-fact reporting style, complete with quoted dialogue between the principal figures. Yet they are not journalistic reports. The earliest of the Gospels, Mark, was probably written about thirty years after Jesus' death. Matthew and Luke borrowed much from Mark and added material they obtained from other sources. By their selection, arrangement, and omissions, the authors of Mark, Matthew, and Luke emphasized what each man felt to be important in the life and death of Jesus.

The author of the Gospel of John, written around the last decade of the first century, was less interested in a straightforward "report" on Jesus' life. The last of the Gospels, John was mostly concerned with the theological significance of Jesus—and did more "editorializing," to borrow a journalistic term for opinionated writing.

If there is general agreement along these lines in New Testament scholarship, then it can be said that differences begin over how much credence can be placed in these accounts of Jesus. Conservative Christian scholars tend to accept the Gospels, the whole Bible, in fact, as error-free or at least basically accurate and factual. Liberal scholars tend to reject the historicity of parts that seem legendary or mythical—such as the narratives about Jesus' birth, much of the miraculous episodes, and often the physical resurrection. The gradations and varieties of biblical interpretation are not all covered by those two characterizations, of course, but that is the background that should be kept in mind when Nag Hammadi findings reach center stage and the debate goes public.

Some attempts to get behind the "editorializing" of John and Paul, and the selective narratives and presuppositions of Mark, Matthew, and Luke, are called quests for the "historical Jesus." What the New Testament historian-theologians come up with is a tentative, limited picture. In fact, as James Robinson points out, the "historical Jesus" is more accurately the "historian's Jesus"—a picture of him and his life reasonably established by historical-critical means.

In this regard scholars have made "considerable progress toward understanding the fantastically creative religious era of which Jesus was a part," said Catholic author-sociologist Andrew M. Greeley, referring to Judaism in the first centuries B.C. and A.D. This kind of research involves little "debunking." "New Testament criticism and New Testament history once may have had a strong flavor of agnostic rationalism about them, and even now each new 'discovery' as reported briefly in the daily papers may be taken by some traditional believers as an attack on their faith. In fact, however, most of the scholars are simply interested in understanding better Jesus and his time."

The search for the historical Jesus includes a comparison of Christian works with other literature from the first centuries. Stories about Jesus and transmission of his sayings were probably by word of mouth in the early years after his crucifixion. But between the time of oral transmission and the New Testament Gospels, "it is beyond doubt" that some written sources existed, declares Helmut Koester of Harvard.

Some scholars detect a collection of parables in the fourth chapter of Mark, presumably taken from a written source. The miracle stories in John are thought to have been derived also from a written source. Well established today is the opinion that "Matthew and Luke both used Mark and a further written source, the so-called synoptic saying source Q," Koester said. Q stands for *Quelle,* the German word for "source." Q is assumed to be a collection of Jesus' sayings, though the document has never been found.

When *The Gospel of Thomas* was discovered among the Nag Hammadi manuscripts, scholars found the closest work yet to Q. Though called a gospel, it is a rather primitive literary piece seemingly designed to preserve the words of Jesus, a wise man, indeed a revealer of divine wisdom. There is no connecting narrative, no life story, no crucifixion or resurrection scenes. It strings together about 114 sayings in more or less random order.

Koester, and other scholars before him, have said that when the New Testament Gospels were written the main purpose was to present the significance of this man-God who suffered, was crucified, and rose again. The traditions about Jesus' words and deeds were incorporated by the Gospel writers, not because of an urge to record his human ministry for history, "but because they serve as parts of a theological introduction to the proclamation of Jesus' passion and death," said Koester. By contrast, someone set down the sayings in *The Gospel of Thomas* for their intrinsic worth rather than as complements to another story.

The editorial peculiarities of Matthew, Mark, and Luke are not recognizable in the proverbial sayings of *Thomas,* Koester says. *Thomas'* source must have been a "very primitive collection of proverbs"—a collection which was incorporated into Q, the common source of Matthew and Luke. These proverbs supplied material in turn for Matthew's "Sermon on the Mount" and Luke's "Sermon on the Plain."

Likewise, the parables in *Thomas* are not taken from the New Testament Gospels but from an earlier source, according to Koester. Four parable-sayings (96, 97, 98, and 109) have no parallels in the New Testament.

If the discovery of previously unknown sayings of Jesus has caused little excitement, it may be because all four are rather cryptic and attempt, like many known parables, to explain the meaning of the "kingdom." Here are two of them (from the Guillaumont, Puech, Quispel, Till, and al Masih translation as are other *Thomas* quotations hereafter):

(96) Jesus [said]: The Kingdom of the Father is like [a] woman, (who) has taken a little leaven [(and) has hidden] it in dough (and) has made large loaves of it. Whoever has ears let him hear.

(98) Jesus said: The Kingdom of the Father is like a man who wishes to kill a powerful man. He drew the sword in his house, he stuck it into the wall, in order to know whether his hand would carry through; then he slew the powerful (man).

Another scholar who has pursued the study of the historical Jesus is Norman Perrin of the University of Chicago. He makes frequent use of *The Gospel of Thomas* in his book, *Rediscovering the Teaching of Jesus*.

"Much of the material in [*Thomas*] has clearly been either modified or created to serve a gnostic Christian purpose," wrote Perrin. But by the same token Christian Gospels also were "either modified or created to serve orthodox Christian purposes."

As a working hypothesis in his search for authentic sayings of Jesus, Perrin assumed, like Koester, that the *Thomas* sayings were from a source independent of Q or Mark, Matthew, and Luke. He says the hypothesis seems to work. For one thing, the sayings attributed to Jesus in *Thomas* do not follow any sequence in the New Testament synoptic Gospels.

Most importantly, Perrin said, "is the fact that over and over again the text of a parable in *Thomas* will be different" from its counterpart in the New Testament—and the *Thomas* form appears to be the more basic, less elaborated version. Because of that, Perrin suggested that the Nag Hammadi text contains examples of Jesus' sayings which are closer to the authentic versions than many found in the New Testament. As an illustration, Perrin cites No. 64, one of the longest "sayings" of Jesus in *The Gospel of Thomas*:

> Jesus said: A man had guest-friends, and when he had pre-pared the dinner, he sent his servant to invite the guest-friends. He went to the first, he said to him: "My master invites thee." He said: "I have some claims against some merchants; they will come to me in the evening; I will go and give them my orders. I pray to be excused from the dinner." He went to another, he said to him: "My master has invited thee." He said to him: "I have bought a house and they request me for a day. I will have no time."
>
> He came to another, he said to him: "My master invites thee." He said to him: "My friend is to be married and I am to arrange a dinner; I shall not be able to come. I pray to be ex-cused from the dinner." He went to another, he said to him: "My master invites thee." He said to him: "I have bought a farm, I go to collect the rent. I shall not be able to come. I pray to be excused."
>
> The servant came, he said to his master: "Those whom thou hast invited to the dinner have excused themselves." The master said to his servant: "Go out to the roads, bring those whom thou shalt find, so that they may dine. Tradesmen and mer-chants [shall] not [enter] the places of my Father.

In the past, Bible commentators had noted the differences in the story as told by Matthew (22:1) and Luke (14:16).

Matthew's feast giver is a king, and the dinner is a marriage feast, symbolizing God and the age to come in Jewish imagery of the time, according to Perrin. Matthew's servants are the Christian "servants of God," but they are rejected, then killed, representing the treatment they received from Jews. The king, angry at this, sends his troops to destroy the city—"certainly a reference to the destruction of Jerusalem by the Romans in-terpreted as the judgment of God upon the Jews, all in ac-cordance with early Christian apologetic," Perrin said. Finally, Matthew adds an epilogue about a guest who came without a wedding garment, that is, he was unprepared for the coming age.

Luke's version is about "a man" who gave a banquet. It tends to shape the story along the themes of his Gospel and the Book of Acts, which he also wrote. The servant is sent out three times—to the original guests (Jews), to the poor and handicapped in the city (Jewish outcasts), and to the persons on the highway outside the city (Gentiles).

"Matthew and Luke have both understood the story as having reference to the missionary situation of the church, and in particular to the situation created by the success of the Gentile mission," Perrin wrote.

It is hard to resist the conclusion, suggests Perrin, that *Thomas'* story of the dinner guests is nearer to the teaching of Jesus than Matthew or Luke. "It does not reflect the situation of the church, nor, except for the generalizing conclusion, is it at all concerned with anything specifically Gnostic." *Thomas'* conclusion—"The tradesmen and merchants [shall] not [enter] the places of my Father"—is taken by Perrin to be a Gnostic rejection of the material world. Noting that stories grow and develop in the telling and retelling, Perrin said *Thomas'* account, except for the excuses and the last sentence, "is in all respects the simplest and least developed version."

Perhaps the shortest saying of Jesus is in *Thomas*—No. 42: "Jesus said: Become passers-by."

Many of Jesus' parables, both in the New Testament Gospels and in *Thomas*, strive to make the point that the kingdom of God is such a surprise and a joy to those who discover it that they abandon less important things and concentrate on the new-found treasure.

The parables about "the treasure in the field" and "the pearl" are just such examples. Matthew placed the two together (13:44–46). *Thomas* has versions of both, but they are widely separated.

Perrin says a previously unknown parable in *Thomas* (No. 8) makes the same point about the kingdom of God:

> And He said: The Man is like a wise fisherman who cast his net into the sea, he drew it up from the sea full of small fish; among them he found a large (and) good fish, that wise fisherman, he threw all the small fish down into the sea, he chose the large fish without regret. Whoever has ears to hear let him hear.

One scholar, Claus-Hunno Hunzinger, says "the Man" can be understood as a gnosticizing substitute for "the kingdom of heaven." Opinion is divided on the "newness" of the parable. Some believe it is not that distinctive, merely *Thomas*' version of the fisherman's "dragnet" parable in Matthew 13:47. But Perrin, with others, considers it a different story.

The debates will continue for years over how many sayings in *The Gospel of Thomas* are "new" sayings of Jesus or closest to the original. At the least, some scholars are already noting the *Thomas* version of sayings along with those of Mark, Matthew, and Luke in New Testament studies.

The picture of Jesus that emerges from analyses such as those of Perrin and Koester is something like this:

The historical Jesus did not proclaim himself Messiah or Son of God. He did not proclaim his so-called Second Coming, but he did proclaim the imminent coming, if not the actual presence, of the kingdom of God. He particularly sympathized with the poor and the unpopular, the latter including the tax collectors and the Samaritans. He shunned fasting and certain other conventions. He called upon his disciples to be alert for the kingdom of God—described really only obliquely through parables—and to dedicate their lives to it, even to the point of breaking family ties.

What his followers thought of him and how they conceived his significance was crucial for the shape of the churches to come. Various concepts influenced the early Christians. Jesus was lord of the future to some, a divine man to those influenced by Hellenistic tendencies to glorify great men, and Wisdom's envoy or Wisdom himself to still others. While all those images are visible in the New Testament, the Gospel writers and Paul emphasized Jesus as the suffering savior who conquered death.

When *The Gospel of Thomas* seems to embellish its reporting of Jesus sayings, the text appears to present Jesus as a wise man, a divine figure, and at times as the embodiment of Wisdom, harking back to the images of Wisdom in Jewish literature. For instance, in *Thomas* 28:

> Jesus said: I took my stand in the midst of the world and in flesh I appeared to them; I found them all drunk, I found none among them athirst. And my soul was afflicted for the sons of men, because they are blind in their heart and do not see that

empty they have come into the world (and that) empty they seek to go out of the world again. But now they are drunk. When they have shaken off their wine, then they will repent.

The Jewish Wisdom of Proverbs, too, came down to the world and attempted to present truth and knowledge to a largely unmindful mankind.

Christian Gnostics tended to emphasize the divine origin and the wisdom-spreading image of Jesus. "Faith is understood as a belief in Jesus' words," says Koester. But otherwise the earthly reality of Jesus becomes incidental when he is linked with the Wisdom myth of descent, revelation, and ascent.

FOURTEEN

The Gnostic Redeemers

Few Christians would find it theologically objectionable for scholars to claim that at times the New Testament describes Jesus as the embodiment of the Wisdom figure in the Old Testament. Jesus was said to "fulfill" the Jewish Scriptures in many ways. But controversial is the suggestion that Jesus was also glorified as a heavenly redeemer in the New Testament under the influence of a Gnostic redeemer myth. Before the Nag Hammadi discovery, such theories of Rudolf Bultmann and others were attacked largely because the myth was reconstructed from the New Testament itself and from later religious texts. Now, the Nag Hammadi library has produced two texts touted as non-Christian and containing myths of a Gnostic redeemer.

Scholarly debate has been rather limited on the subject, but when the Nag Hammadi library becomes easily accessible, the question of the Gnostic redeemers and their possible relationship to the Christian image of Jesus will probably focus on two treatises, *The Paraphrase of Shem* and *The Apocalypse of Adam*.

The savior in *The Paraphrase of Shem* is Derdekeas, the "son of the undefiled, infinite Light." Shem is the mortal to whom Derdekeas reveals his story. Derdekeas does battle with Darkness, Mother Nature, and a giant womb in his efforts to rescue

Spirit and the "Mind" of Darkness. "What becomes immediately apparent is that we have here in one form or other the features which have long been suspected by many New Testament scholars to be outside influences on New Testament Christology," said Frederik Wisse.

In summarizing the features of Derdekeas which are relevant to Jesus, Wisse wrote:

> The redeemer is the son and likeness of the perfect Light, in substance equivalent to the Christian concept of the preexistent son of God. Moved by pity, he descends to the realm of evil to save the fallen light of the Spirit, which is the root and origin of the race of Shem. During his stay in Hades he experiences the hostility of the powers of Darkness and goes unrecognized. He puts on "the beast," which seems to be the body, and in that disguise advances the work of salvation, which is a cosmic event. After his stay on earth he receives honor from his garments. Finally, he reveals his saving work as the life-giving Gnosis to his elect.

According to *The Paraphrase of Shem*, everything had been fine in primordial times among the universe's three "roots"— the supreme Light full of reason . . . the evil Darkness who wraps the Mind in a chaotic fire . . . and the Spirit who was "a gentle, humble light."

Only when Darkness spied the remarkable Spirit did he realize he was not the only power around. (Darkness was still completely unaware of the supreme Light.) Darkness sought to become equal to the Spirit, but as in much Gnostic myth making, the forces of ignorance and evil can never capture or become like the purer forces of the universe.

The Paraphrase of Shem contains a complex series of events, making the narrative hard to follow. Sample the cataclysmic scope of the storytelling at the point where the womb is formed:

> And from the Darkness the water became a cloud. And from the cloud the womb took shape. The chaotic fire, which was a deviation, went there. And when the Darkness saw it he became unclean. And when he had aroused (himself), he rubbed the womb. His mind dissolved down to the depths of Nature. It mingled with the power of the Darkness' bitterness. And (Nature's) eye ruptured from the malady . . .

Sexual imagery is woven throughout the narrative. There was the time when Derdekeas, otherwise very powerful, was unable to speak in the cloud of the hymen. "Frightful was the (hymen's) fire, since it exalted itself without humility . . ."

Entering the lower regions, Derdekeas wore an assortment of garments, at one point exchanging a luminous one for one of fire prior to an encounter with Nature. (She is not called "Mother Nature" in the text, but she is a feminine being and has some of the characteristics one might associate with the legendary Mother Nature at her worst.) Derdekeas rubbed against Nature with his garment, causing the "wrathful womb" to come up and for the Mind of Darkness to be cast off. This loss disturbed her so much that she began to cry. "In her tears," Derdekeas continued, "she cast off the power of the Spirit."

Later, Derdekeas "put on the beast" and stood in front of the womb. "I put before her a great request, that a heaven and an earth may come into being in order that the whole light may rise up." "Mother" Nature, thinking the request came from one of her animal sons, blows upon the water. The heaven was created, and from the residue of the heaven, the earth came into being.

Derdekeas returned to Nature another time, compelling forms within her to rub their tongues with each other and to copulate: "They begot winds and demons, and the power which is from the fire, the Darkness and the Spirit." Derdekeas directed the Mind to reign over the winds and demons and gave the Mind a measure of majesty to be independently strong "in order that at the end of time when Nature will be destroyed, he may rest in the honored place."

The foregoing reference to the "end of time" is typical of Jewish apocalyptic literature as well as the framework of *The Paraphrase of Shem*. The text opened with Shem telling how his mind was snatched from his body and carried to the top of creation. The voice of Derdekeas told him of the primordial conflicts and the creation of earth, then informed Shem that he and his race are a mixture of the forces above—a part of the winds and demons, and also a mind imbued with light.

Shem is warned about a demon, later called Soldas, who will bring a flood to try to wipe out his race. As in *The Na-*

ture of the Archons and *On the Origin of the World,* primeval biblical events have been given an evil meaning. In *The Paraphrase of Shem,* a "tower," apparently the Tower of Babel, is mentioned favorably and so is Sodom.

Derdekeas tells Shem to "proclaim quickly to the Sodomites your universal teaching, for they are your members." The Sodomites will then rest with a pure conscience, but even so, "Sodom will be burned unjustly by a base Nature."

The demon, comparable but not identical to the Gnostic Creator God, will come to a river to baptize "erroneously . . . with an incomplete baptism." Water baptism is considered wrong by *Paraphrase's* author.

The objection to water baptism is puzzling, but Epiphanius wrote of an early Gnostic sect, the Archontici, who despised the rite. The Archontici supposedly lived in Palestine and were related to the Sethians.

Hippolytus, onetime bishop of Rome, described a document somewhat similar to *The Paraphrase of Shem,* which had been Christianized. The scene of the redeemer before the womb was reworked into the incarnation of Christ, that is, Christ putting on the body of Jesus. Hippolytus called the work *The Paraphrase of Seth.* Scholars suspect that the names Seth and Shem may have been interchanged in Gnostic circles and that the two documents are related.

The Paraphrase of Shem, as it appears in the Nag Hammadi library, however, seems to be a non-Christian treatise which made use of and radically transformed Old Testament materials, according to Wisse.

Paraphrase, says Pheme Perkins, apparently reused some mythic images of divine warriors known in the ancient Near East. The storm god, whether the Caananites' Ba'al or the Jewish Yahweh, made earthly entrances accompanied by thunder, lightning, and earthquakes. "These motifs recur in association with the appearance of the revealer in chaos in *The Apocryphon of John* and the *Trimorphic Protennoia,*" she said. "Both works use a scheme in which the revealer descends into the world three times. The first two cause destruction in chaos." By coming in human form the third time, the revealer avoids these circumstances.

But the "divine warrior" of ancient Near East lore becomes

a "revealer" in the Gnostic stories, including *Paraphrase*. "Actual battles or even effective contact between the revealer and his demonic opponents never take place," Perkins points out. She calls Derdekeas and other such figures "revealers" rather than "redeemers." Is the distinction real? To the Gnostics, being awakened from their sleep and perceiving the knowledge, "gnosis," of their beginnings and destiny was "redeeming" for them. In other words, obtaining mystical knowledge of this kind was thought to be their salvation, and in that sense a revealer-figure was also a redeemer.

Christians have believed that Jesus Christ brought saving knowledge to humanity. But since he was also crucified, and the meaning of this event must be explained, his death also was seen as a redeeming act—"He died for our sins."

The Nag Hammadi library contains a number of mythical revealer-redeemer figures, often identified vaguely or directly with Jesus. That is not surprising, considering the fact that most texts had undergone rewriting and revision under the impact of Christianity.

Is it irreverent of some New Testament scholars to search for early myths of a heavenly redeemer who descends to the earth with knowledge for mortals, then ascends back to the light, as if this was needed to explain Christianity's description of Jesus in those terms? Traditional Christians would maintain that Christ was said to have descended to earth and returned to heaven simply because he did in fact do that.

"The more critical thinker" would ask where this religious symbolism came from, suggests James M. Robinson. "The Nag Hammadi Codices have produced the missing documentation. *The Apocalypse of Adam*, a non-Christian Jewish Gnostic interpretation of Genesis, presents the redeemer as coming to earth, suffering and triumphing." Robinson asserts that the text seems to have been written in the Syrian-Jordan region during the first century A.D.

The Apocalypse of Adam, written as if Adam was prophesying future calamities to his son Seth, said the wrathful Creator God would first seek to destroy Seth's descendants by means of a flood, then by fire, sulphur, and asphalt (see chap. 12). Angels would rescue them in those two cases, but a third threat of judgment would be handled by the Illuminator.

And he will redeem their souls from the day of death. For the whole creation which came from the dead earth will be under the authority of death. But those who reflect upon the knowledge of the eternal God in their heart will not perish.

The Illuminator is a "man," as the text indicates:

And he will perform signs and wonders in order to scorn their powers and their Archons.

The God of the powers will be disturbed, saying: "What is the power of this man who is higher than we?" Then he will arouse a great wrath against that man.

And the glory will withdraw and dwell in the holy houses which it has chosen for itself. And the powers will not see it with their eyes, nor will they see the Illuminator either.

Then they will punish the flesh of the man upon whom the holy spirit has come.

The Archon and fellow powers will wonder about the origin of the scornful Illuminator. The *Apocalypse* lists thirteen erroneous explanations given by thirteen "kingdoms." The fourteenth—"the generation without a king," the Gnostic one—contends that the highest God chose the Illuminator to be his agent of knowledge. "The seed of all those who will receive his name upon the water will fight against the power" of the Creator God.

In *The Apocalypse of Adam* "we have a clearly developed redeemer-myth which is at once Gnostic and without any reference to Jesus as the Gnostic redeemer or his prototype," wrote George MacRae in a 1965 article.

MacRae noted that Bohlig concluded that the work was an example of "pre-Christian Gnosticism." Actually, some scholars have since decided that "non-Christian Gnosticism" may be the best term, one referring either to a text composed chronologically before Christ or before the start of Christian preaching and influence.

Is a Christian influence betrayed by the fact that the Illuminator performs "signs and wonders" and suffers in the flesh, and that his followers receive "his name upon the water?" MacRae resisted such arguments, both in his 1965 article and in a 1972 seminar. To borrow Christian ideas or expressions and then eliminate any clear reference to Christ or another New Testament personality, he said, would have been contrary to the pattern of the Gnostic writers in the Nag Hammadi texts.

Another Nag Hammadi manuscript, *The Concept of Our Great Power*, might appear to ruin that argument, but MacRae says it doesn't: "This text contains a comparatively detailed account of the future coming of Jesus without any trace of Christian names." But there is little doubt that the New Testament is known and drawn upon, he said. The one who is to come "will speak in parables," he is "betrayed" by "one of those who followed him," and his "word annulled the law of the age."

By comparison, MacRae said he found no explicit or veiled Christian allusions in *The Apocalypse of Adam*. He believes the tribulation of the Illuminator to be drawn from the images of the suffering servant in Isaiah, not from Jesus' suffering. "The point is that the early Christian preaching did not invent the notion of a suffering religious leader out of whole cloth." An interesting parallel to the suffering Illuminator, he said, is the Dead Sea Scrolls' venerated righteous teacher, a revealer-figure who was persecuted by opposing powers.

Both *The Paraphrase of Shem* and *The Apocalypse of Adam* draw on sections of Genesis for mythical formulas, and both insert into their stories a Gnostic redeemer who cannot be seen as fashioned after Jesus Christ. "More nearly the reverse is true," said Robinson. "These texts demonstrate the mythological wealth that offbeat Judaism made available to nascent Christianity for expressing the grandeur of Jesus."

Remarkably, the Nag Hammadi discovery sheds light, not only on the historical Jesus (in *The Gospel of Thomas*), but also on the mythical interpretations of Jesus that were incorporated in the New Testament.

FIFTEEN

Jesus—The Light of the World

The Nag Hammadi manuscripts frequently show how the world would remember Jesus today if the Gnostic view had prevailed in the early Christian years. After the crucifixion, Jesus reappeared on earth only as a bright light, according to Gnostic accounts.

Jesus' disciples were walking up the Mount of Olives where they had gathered in the days when Christ "was in the body." In this scene from Nag Hammadi's *The Letter of Peter to Philip* the disciples went up the hill to pray and arriving, threw themselves on their knees.

The disciples prayed first to the "Father of the Light," father of the holy child Jesus Christ who became for them "an illuminator" in the darkness.·

In a second prayer they appealed: "Son of Life, Son of Immortality who is in the light, Son, Christ of Immortality, our Redeemer, give us power, for they seek to kill us."

A great light appeared, so bright that the mountain was bathed in brilliance. A voice called out to the disciples: "Listen to my words, for I am going to speak to you. What are you concerned about? I am Jesus Christ, who is with you forever."

Thus, Christ returns in *The Letter of Peter to Philip* to aid and comfort the disciples—not in bodily form, but as a voice within a bright light. In the Christian Gnostic view, this occurrence would be only natural. The Father and the Son are intimately connected with the divine Light above; indeed, they are the Light.

In *The Apocryphon of John,* a Pharisee tells John that the Nazarene who taught him was a deceiver, turning him from the tradition of his fathers. Perturbed, John heads toward the Mount of Olives, wondering about the origin of the Savior and other questions.

"Immediately, as I thought about these things, the heavens opened," according to John. "The entire creation lit up with an (unearthly) light, and the (entire) cosmos trembled."

As John falls down with fear, a child suddenly appears to him in the light. The form at first seemed to be that of an old person, then a "little one." Several forms began coalescing in the light, and John detected three, apparently transparent forms. Christ's voice speaks to him from the light, and a dialogue is launched in *The Apocryphon of John.*

At first glance, such accounts might strike the modern reader as completely foreign to the New Testament understanding of Jesus' resurrection appearances. The Gospels indicated that the resurrected Christ had a body as humanlike as he had possessed before his crucifixion. Though he sometimes disguises himself or appears and vanishes like a magical spirit, for the most part his fleshly reappearances are emphasized. (The supernatural side of the resurrected Christ necessarily reappears at his ascension to heaven in the New Testament.)

The earliest Christian narratives of the resurrection, however, may have presented the returned Christ as a bright light much as the Gnostic writings did, Robinson suggests. New Testament studies have conjectured that a bright-light resurrection was rejected by early Christian writers because it "ultimately came to seem too ghostly, too much like the resurrection appearances claimed by emerging Gnosticism," Robinson said.

As a result that kind of story was either suppressed or put back into the lifetime of Jesus where it could not be considered a resurrection scene—such as the transfiguration episode (see Matt. 17:1–8, Mark 9:2–8, Luke 9:28–36). The story opens with Jesus leading Peter, James, and John up a high mountain. Suddenly, Jesus is "transfigured" before them.

"His face shone like the sun, and his garments became white as light," says Matthew. Moses and Elijah appear to talk with Jesus; then a voice comes from a "bright cloud" above them, saying, "This is my beloved Son, with whom I am well pleased; listen to him."

The apostle Paul, who wrote his Letters before the Gospels were composed, maintained that he witnessed a genuine resurrection appearance of Christ even though it was not a bodily one. Paul encountered a blinding light on the road to Damascus. The voice from the light identified itself as Jesus and rebuked Paul for persecuting the Christians. The New Testament's Book of Acts places Paul's conversion-encounter outside the forty-day period of resurrection appearances, however, as if to classify Paul's experience as an exception.

In the Book of Revelation, also known as The Apocalypse of John, Jesus appears as a white-haired, robed wonder with eyes like flames of fire and a face shining like the sun at full strength (Rev. 1:12–16). Robinson claims this also describes a resurrection appearance but that it is "cast in such lurid, mythological language that it is often overlooked."

While the developing church may have substituted the humanlike appearances for such voice-from-the-light visions, the Gnostics continued to record resurrection scenes in the luminous tradition, which better suited their mystical, otherworldly theology. The stories become full-blown in Gnostic hands.

Traditional Christians may care little about the Gnostic rendering except that, if the trajectory is reversed, what "was going on in the background of the New Testament itself" can be seen, to use Robinson's words.

SIXTEEN

The Laughing Jesus

Most Gnostics apparently believed that Jesus did not suffer on the cross inasmuch as he was in the body only as long as he wished. They claimed that at the last moment Jesus deceived his ignorant enemies and laughed at their blindness.

The Nag Hammadi discovery contains two versions of that incredible story. Significantly, the laughing Jesus is a successor to several mocking saviors encountered in Gnostic texts.

One of Nag Hammadi's laughing Jesus scenes is contained in *The Apocalypse of Peter* where the disciple Peter is sitting in a temple, learning some of the divine mysteries from the Savior. A vision comes to Peter about a crowd approaching and seizing the Lord. "What do I see, O Lord?" asks Peter desperately. "Who is this above the tree (the cross), who is happy and laughs? Is it another whose feet and hands they are striking?"

The Savior replies to Peter: "He whom you see above the tree, glad and laughing, is the living Jesus. But the one into whose hands and feet they drive the nails is his fleshly part, which is the substitute . . . one made in his likeness."

Only the bodily Jesus is being murdered, *The Apocalypse of Peter* explains. The persecutors are unaware that a separation has taken place and that the real Jesus, now called the "living Savior," stands by unseen. "Because of this he laughs at their lack of perception, knowing that they are born blind."

The Apocalypse of Peter's author "disdainfully rejects those who cling to a dead man; i.e., the crucified physical Jesus, and presents the savior as the revealer of life-giving *gnosis*," said James Brashler.

A somewhat similar "laughing Jesus" crucifixion scene appears in another Nag Hammadi Gnostic text, *The Second Treatise of the Great Seth*. The speaker, presumably Jesus Christ, tells of the folly of his would-be executioners:

> It was not I whom they struck with the reed. It was another who lifted the cross onto his shoulders—Simon. It was another on whose head they placed the thorny crown. But I was up above, rejoicing over all the wealth of the archons and the offspring of the error of their empty glory. And I was laughing at their ignorance.

Until the discovery of the Nag Hammadi library, the Gnostic story of a laughing Jesus who eludes the crucifixion was known only from Irenaeus and Epiphanius. The two church leaders attributed the story to a Gnostic teacher named Basilides, who was described as active during the reign of Roman emperor Antoninus Pius (A.D. 117–138).

A prolific writer, Basilides was said to have composed, among other things, a psalm book and a gospel. Basilides had elaborate teachings, Irenaeus said, "so that he may appear to have discovered something higher and more like the truth."

Basilides' system began with the Father, from whom came *Nous* ("mind" or "rational thought"), who begat *Logos* ("word" or "reason"), followed by a series of forces, powers, and angels until 365 heavens were created. The God of the Jews was chief among the angels of the lowest heaven. Seeing that the Jewish God tried to subjugate people of other nations, the Father sent his first-born Nous—who is called the Christ—to liberate people from the powers who formed the world.

Here is Basilides' story of the crucifixion escape, as told by Irenaeus:

> . . . He did not suffer, but a certain Simon of Cyrene was compelled to carry his cross for him; and this (Simon) was transformed by him (Jesus) so that he was thought to be Jesus himself, and was crucified through ignorance and error. Jesus,

however, took on the form of Simon, and stood by laughing at them.

For since he was an incorporeal power and the Nous of the unborn Father, he was transformed in whatever way he pleased, and in this way he ascended to him who had sent him, laughing at them, since he could not be held and was invisible to all. Therefore, those who know these things have been set free from the rulers who made this world.

Thus, says Irenaeus in summarizing Basilides' creed, if anyone confesses the crucified Jesus, "he is still a slave" and under the power of the worldly archons.

Irenaeus may be right in saying Basilides spread that version of the crucifixion, but scholars suspect it was current among many Gnostics, perhaps even before Basilides' time. Whether Simon was substituted or Jesus merely separated from his body, *The Second Treatise of the Great Seth,* Basilides' account, and *The Apocalypse of Peter* all describe the Savior above the cross, laughing at the ignorance or blindness of the executioners.

But why was the Savior laughing? Jesus laughs nowhere in the New Testament. Robert M. Grant said the answer may be provided by words from Psalm 2, which was held to be meaningful by early Christians. The psalm tells of "rulers" or "archons" conspiring "against the Lord and his Anointed." But, the psalm continues, "He who sits in the heavens laughs; the Lord has them in derision." Grant says that this may be the source for the notion that the Savior derided his enemies.

The idea that the deity would laugh at earthly evildoers also could be supported by a line in Psalm 59—"But thou, O Lord, dost laugh at them; thou dost hold all the nations in derision."

Yet another Old Testament image is important here. The figure of Wisdom ("Sophia") in Proverbs has been cited by Bultmann as a key to the Gnostic redeemer concept. Once residing with God on high, Wisdom comes down to earth and attempts to spread her knowledge. She warns those who scorn her that she will laugh at and mock them when calamity comes.

The mocking idea is carried over in *The Nature of the Archons* and *On the Origin of the World.* In those Gnostic writings, Sophia and Eve, her daughter, both patterned after Wisdom in the Jewish literature, mock the archons.

Eve is pursued by the lustful archons in both texts, but she laughs at their senselessness and blindness. She fools them by providing a substitute image of herself for them to rape. Just so, the living Jesus in later stories provides a substitute for the archons to crucify!

Sophia Zoe also laughs at the archons' desire to create a man in *On the Origin of the World.* She laughs because she knows they are blind. And when it was evident to the chief Archon's minions that there was a higher realm, they laughed at the Archon for saying he was God and that no one existed before him.

The Illuminator in *The Apocalypse of Adam,* it is predicted, will perform signs and wonders in order to scorn the archons.

Laughter is found in *The Second Treatise of the Great Seth* in more than just the crucifixion scene. At one point, the Creator God bellows: "I am God, and there is no other beside me." The narrator, later identified with Jesus Christ, reacts: "I laughed in joy when I examined his empty glory." *Great Seth* also embodies a remarkable "laughing-stock" section which hints that mockery might have been employed in some Gnostic liturgy. The Archon "was a laughing-stock" not only because he said he was God and there was no other, but also because he was a jealous God who brought the sins of the fathers onto the sons for three and four generations. Adam, Abraham, Isaac, Jacob, David, Solomon, Moses, the twelve prophets, and John the Baptist were all "laughing-stocks," says the text in a series of seven recitations, all ending with a refrain stating the innocence of the readers.

"A very patterned piece, the laughing-stock section gives the appearance of a litany (more accurately, a counter-litany)," said Joseph A. Gibbons. "This type of consistent pattern is unique in *Great Seth.* Although concentrating on Old Testament figures, the piece is a product of Christian gnosticism for the Old Testament extends from 'Adam to Moses to John the Baptist.' It fits the general attitude of *Great Seth*—disdain for the orthodox who worship a lesser god."

If Gibbons is correct in assigning a "fairly late date in the history of Christian gnosticism" for the *Great Seth,* it would probably be correct to say that mockery was an attitudinal trait, perhaps even a tactic, of some Gnostics for much of their history.

Not all laughter in the Nag Hammadi texts is scornful. Reacting to a question from John in *The Apocryphon of John,* Jesus "laughed" and then gave his reply. In *The Sophia of Jesus Christ,* Jesus greets his disciples by saying, "Peace." But the disciples wondered and were afraid. "The Savior laughed and said to them, 'What are you thinking about? What is perplexing you?'"

A serious tone prevails in the gospels and other New Testament writings. "As it should be," most Christians might respond. But if Jesus' humanity is an important part of orthodox Christianity, would not a smiling or laughing Jesus have contributed to his humanness? Apparently the Gospel writers and others did not wish to risk the connotations that laughter can assume—mockery in some cases, frivolity in other instances.

It must be admitted, however, that the jovial Jesus of the Gnostics was less human than the New Testament versions. The Gnostics generally held a "docetic" view of Jesus Christ—that he didn't really suffer on the cross and did not therefore need to be raised from the dead. The "laughing Jesus" in two Nag Hammadi texts probably demonstrates the docetic view most dramatically.

While the Gnostics most often considered Jesus' body a mere garment, the diversity of thought within Gnosticism also included an orthodox minority.

A strong statement affirming Jesus' human qualities and his physical suffering on the cross appears in Nag Hammadi's *Melchizedek.* The passage tells of the encounter of "Jesus Christ, the Son of God" with hostile powers who will initiate false charges against him:

> (They) will come in his name and they will say of him that he is unbegotten though he has been begotten, (that) he does not eat even though he eats, (that) he does not drink even though he drinks, (that) he is uncircumcised though he has been circumcised, (that) he is unfleshly though he has come in the flesh (that) he did not come to suffering, (though) he came to suffering, (that) he did not rise from the dead (though) he arose from (the) dead.

James M. Robinson (left) and Birger Pearson of the University of California, Santa Barbara, with the Codex I cover purchased by the Institute for Antiquity and Christianity, Claremont, Calif., at which much of the English-language translation and analysis of the library is coordinated.—Claremont Graduate School

Birger Pearson says that some Gnostic writings seem to take ambiguous stances on whether Jesus suffered or not but that *Melchizedek*'s assertions are "unyieldingly nonparadoxical. Such a stance is most unusual in a gnostic document, indeed unparalleled." The treatise *is* Gnostic, he said, inasmuch as there are references to archons, authorities, and other Gnostic characters plus a reference to the elect people as "the congregation of the children of Seth."

It may be possible to link this writing to a sect called the Melchizedekians, says Pearson. (Both Melchizedek, the ancient Canaanite priest-king of the Old Testament, and Jesus were accorded central roles in the text.) The Melchizedekians were said to believe in the true humanity of Christ.

One of the surprises to emerge from the Nag Hammadi library has been such orthodox or near-orthodox expressions of Christianity. Some of these texts came from the school of Valentinus, the Gnostic who came close to changing a bit of church history.

THE GNOSTIC
PHENOMENON

SEVENTEEN

Valentinus, the Formidable Gnostic

Sometime in the middle of the second century, church authorities held an election for a new bishop of Rome, and the loser was a brilliant religious thinker, an Egyptian born and educated man with a Latin name, Valentinus.

The man chosen bishop over Valentinus was referred to in sketchy historical accounts as a "martyr"—possibly Pius, who became pope about A.D. 143. Or possibly the winner was Anicetus, whose episcopacy of Rome extended from about A.D. 154 to A.D. 165. At any rate, "Valentinus came to Rome in the time of Hyginus, flourished under Pius, and remained until Anicetus," reported Irenaeus.

Valentinus founded a school of thought branded by Irenaeus as multiheaded and bewildering. "Every day everyone of them invents something new, and none of them is considered perfect unless he is productive in this way." One of Valentinus' best-known disciples was Ptolemaeus, whose pupil Heracleon, wrote the first systematic exegesis, or interpretation, of the Gospel of John.

Churchman Tertullian, of a later generation than Valentinus, said Valentinus and another heretic, Marcion, had been "cast out [of the church] once and again." Historical evidence is too skimpy to know whether Valentinus turned more Gnostic after losing the election, or whether he lost the election because of his Gnostic view of Christianity.

Tertullian had grudging admiration for Valentinus ". . . because both as to talent and eloquence he was an able man." Another church father, Jerome, had a backhand compliment for Valentinus, too. "No one can bring a heresy into being unless he is possessed, by nature, of an outstanding intellect and has gifts provided by God. Such a person was Valentinus."

Valentinus and his disciples drew more critical comment from church fathers than any other Gnostic group. As a result, Christian scholars in later centuries were able to put together a rough idea of Valentinian Gnosticism. The long descriptions by Irenaeus and others of Valentinianism have persuaded scholars that Gnosticism had its primary intellectual flowering in second-century Valentinian writings.

Thus, it was with great relish that researchers looked forward to studying the likely Valentinian texts in the Nag Hammadi collection, which, perhaps for no special reason, includes relatively few Valentinian works.

Some scholars believe at least one tractate, *The Gospel of Truth*, may have been composed by Valentinus himself. Surprisingly, it contains few obvious references to the Valentinian mythology described by church fathers.

That mythology was summarized nicely by Hans Jonas in *The Gnostic Religion*. In the beginning was the Fore-Father or Abyss, entirely incomprehensible. With him was Silence, also called Grace or Thought. When the Abyss decided to conceive, Silence brought forth Mind, who alone could comprehend the greatness of the Fore-Father.

Mind is also called the Only-Begotten and Father. With him, Truth (a feminine word) was produced, thus forming two original male-female pairs: Abyss (m.) and Silence (f.), Mind (m.) and Truth (f.).

Then Mind, together with his consort, projected the pair Word (m.) and Life (f.). From them was emitted Man (m.) and Church (f.). These eight entities constituted what the Valentinians called the Ogdoad. The last two pairs, wishing to glorify the Father, produced more emanations. This led to the completion of the thirty aeons which make up the Pleroma, literally, the "Fullness" of divine entities.

The last feminine figure in the chain is Sophia, who leapt farthest. She made a passionate attempt to find, or comprehend, the Father, but because it was impossible, she fell into great agony. She was stopped in her quest by a power called Limit. Limit reconciled her to her inability to comprehend the Father, but left behind were her expended passions, a formless entity the Valentinians sometimes called an "abortion."

The other aeons, disturbed by Sophia's sighs over her abortion, appealed to the Father for help. The unknowable one produced a new pair—Christos and the Holy Spirit. Christos brings calm to the aeon hierarchy and also puts form into the abortion which was necessarily cast out of the Pleroma. That form becomes the so-called "lower Sophia," or Achamoth (from the Hebrew word for "wisdom," *hokhmah*).

The lower Sophia is outside the Light and the Pleroma, but she nevertheless seeks it. Alone in the outer darkness she is subjected to every kind of suffering imaginable.

"Now she wept and grieved because she was left alone in the Darkness and the Void," according to Irenaeus. But when she thought of the Light "she became cheerful and laughed," only to fall again into fear and bewilderment.

Jonas says the lower Sophia "repeats on her own level the scale of emotions which her mother in the Pleroma underwent, the only difference being that these passions now pass over into the form of definitive states of being, and as such they can become the substance of the world."

The mechanics of this creation were made possible by the aeon Jesus, who was formed from the calmed unity of the Pleroma. Christos could not leave the Pleroma, but Jesus was sent both as the consort of the lower Sophia and as her savior, that is, one who would free her from her passions.

The lower Sophia's pleas resulted in the creation of the Creator God (called the Demiurge in Valentinianism) and everything pertaining to human souls. From the rest of the lower Sophia's passions came the basic materials of the cosmos: from her tears, the water; from her laughter, the luminaries (sun and stars); from her grief and shock, the more solid elements of the world. (Laughter in this version of Valentinianism by Irenaeus is associated with happy thoughts of light!)

Three human elements were derived from the experiences

of the lower Sophia, and they are important in understanding the salvation message of the Valentinian Gnostics. The human body was the result of her passions; the soul came from her pleas; and the spirit, from the reception of light from her savior. Humans, aware of their bodies and souls but not of the divine light or spirit in themselves, finally are rescued after the aeon Jesus descends on the human Jesus at his baptism in the Jordan River. This divinely infilled Jesus then spreads the gnosis to mankind. The spirits in humans, saved by this knowledge, are ultimately destined to enter the Pleroma with their "Mother," the lower Sophia.

"According to Gnostic ideas," says Jan Zandee of the Netherlands, "sin is ignorance and salvation is the imparting of true knowledge concerning God. But the basis of ignorance lies in God himself, since by virtue of his nature He is unknowable." The supreme God, in other words, emanates aspects of himself that are deficient (except for the only-begotten Mind) in that they don't know the Father. "The further from the source of light, the blacker is the darkness of ignorance in which the creature lives," said Zandee.

There is a philosophical need to distinguish between the unity of the Pleroma and the inadequacies of the world, and it can be seen also in texts of the Valentinian school in the Nag Hammadi library. "The aeons (of the Pleroma) were not cut off from the Father, but he spreads out over them," says *The Tripartite Tractate*. "Strong is the system of the Pleroma; small is that which broke loose (and) became the world," says *The Treatise on the Resurrection.*

Irenaeus was right when he said the Valentinians had many variations on a theme, the basic unchanging motif being that man's origins are from the unknowable Light above which is far removed from the murky ignorance of the cosmos. Different writers chose different aeons, or aspects, of the Father to play important roles in the saving of mankind.

The Word (*Logos*) of God is considered a salvation force, a function of the highest God, in *The Tripartite Tractate*. That, of course, is similar to the Fourth Gospel's identification of Jesus Christ as the Word of God.

The Word as the Savior is also presented in the opening of *The Gospel of Truth*, a Valentinian treatise that is one of the most translated and written about texts from Nag Hammadi. It begins:

> The gospel of truth is a joy for those who have received from the Father of truth the favor of knowing him through the power of the Word that came forth from the Pleroma—the one who is in the thought and the mind of the Father; that is, the one who is addressed as the Savior . . .

Some of the scholars who believe the author of *The Gospel of Truth* was Valentinus himself include W. C. van Unnik, Kendrick Grobel, and Robert M. Grant. The latter conjectured that Valentinus wrote it about A.D. 150 in Rome just before his final expulsion from the church.

Grobel favored Valentinus as the author even though there are so-called Valentinian elements missing from *The Gospel of Truth*. The Nag Hammadi text has no detailed list of aeons, no split between a Christ and a Jesus, no mention of a Demiurge—no distinction between a good and an evil God. Most striking is the absence of Sophia, but some believe her place is taken by "Error" in a kind of substitute myth.

Error appears early in *The Gospel of Truth* in passages that seem to hark back to Sophia's anguish and attempts to comprehend the Father:

> Ignorance of the Father brought about anguish and terror. And anguish grew solid like a fog so that no one was able to see. For this reason Error became powerful; she fashioned her own matter in emptiness, not having known the truth.

George MacRae asserts that "because this account is of itself not readily intelligible without a knowledge of the Sophia myth, one may conclude that *The Gospel of Truth* is a later formulation which presupposes the earlier, perhaps less sophisticated, myth." Hans Jonas likewise thought that it is more plausible for a philosophical abstraction to follow the detailed myth.

That progression from detailed myth making to sophisticated commentary—at least in the early stages of Gnosticism—would support conjecture that texts such as *The Apocryphon of John*, with its long discussions of aeons, were composed in their original forms before the time of Valentinus.

The Gospel of Truth certainly displays an intellectual flair to match the church fathers' praise of Valentinus. The text maintains the revelations of Jesus Christ led to the discovery by mortals of the truth within themselves.

> He was nailed to a tree; he became a fruit of the knowledge of the Father, which did not, however, become destructive because it was eaten, but to those who ate it, it gave (cause) to become glad in the discovery . . . They discovered him in themselves—the incomprehensible, inconceivable one, the Father, the perfect one . . .

The meditations in *The Gospel of Truth,* certainly not a gospel in the New Testament sense, are wordy, ambiguous, or vague for stretches at a time. But interspersed among these are lines about the Savior that would have been a credit to the most orthodox Christian writer.

> Light spoke through his mouth, and his voice gave birth to life. He gave them thought and understanding, and mercy and salvation, and the spirit of power from the infiniteness and gentleness of the Father . . .
> He became a way for those who were lost and knowledge for those who were ignorant, a discovery for those who were searching, and a strengthening for those who were wavering, immaculateness for those who were defiled.

A charitable concern might be read into the following:

> Make firm the foot of those who have stumbled and stretch out your hand to those who are ill. Feed those who are hungry and give repose to those who suffer, and raise up those who wish to rise, and awaken those who sleep.

However, a Gnostic would understand the foregoing to mean that true knowledge should be provided to those who hunger for the truth. Awakening the ignorant from their "sleep" is common Gnostic theme.

Once this knowledge is obtained, did Gnostics consider themselves saved? Some Nag Hammadi manuscripts seem to support earlier scholarly surmises that the Gnostics usually believed they became the elect and had already earned a sure spot in the highest heaven or even ascended to heaven in a spiritual sense.

The Gospel of Truth seems to confirm this: "Hence, if one has knowledge, he is from above. If he is called, he hears, he replies, and he turns toward him who called him and he ascends to him and knows what he is called."

The author of *The Treatise on the Resurrection* even quotes Paul to support this idea: "Then, indeed, as the Apostle said, 'We suffered with him, and we rose with him, and we went to heaven with him.'"

EIGHTEEN

Orgy Lovers?
Women Haters?

Besides being considered one of the worst heresies experienced by Christianity for some eighteen hundred years, Gnosticism has borne the stigma long after its demise of a religious philosophy which induced believers into lives of debauchery. Some Gnostic sects, said contemporaneous opponents, engaged in sexual orgies under the pretext of participating in a sacred ritual.

If there were ever any Gnostic writings that justified such attitudes, they are not to be found in the Nag Hammadi Gnostic Library. Some treatises indicate a disregard for the values of this world by saying there is no evil and no good, but no sanction for amoral behavior is plainly stated. Some writings, in fact, indicate that ascetic withdrawal is the most desirable response to the lusts of the world.

No Nag Hammadi document has been identified with the philosophy of Simon Magus, his whore-companion Helena, and his love-potion-concocting priests.

Some texts describe a mysterious bridal chamber, but it apparently was not used in the manner of which the Gnostic Marcus was accused by Irenaeus. The Church father said Marcus was a self-proclaimed prophet and magician who would pray over a cup of purple liquid mixed with wine, a concoction Marcus said was the blood of Grace, the aeon also known as Silence in the Valentinian Pleroma.

Marcus would have a woman taste of the cup and allow Grace to flow into her. "He concerns himself in particular with women, especially with those of high rank, the elegantly attired and wealthy, whom he frequently attempts to lead astray by flattering them and saying, 'I desire to make thee a partaker of my Grace . . .'"

Marcus suggested that the way to do that was to come together, said Irenaeus. "'. . . Adorn thyself as a bride who expects her bridegroom, that thou mayest be what I am, and I what thou art. Receive in thy bridechamber the seed of light. Receive from me the bridegroom, and give him a place, and have a place in him. Behold, Grace has descended upon thee; open thy mouth and prophesy.'"

If the woman replies, "I have never prophesied before, nor can I prophesy," then Marcus offers some more prayers and exhorts her to try again.

The woman, "deluded and puffed up by what has been said," according to Irenaeus, takes the risk and heart pounding, she utters "ridiculous nonsense," anything that comes into her head. Convinced by Marcus that she is a prophetess, she profusely thanks him for sharing Grace with her.

"She tries to repay him, not only with a gift of her possessions—by which he has collected a great deal of money—but also by physical intercourse, prepared as she is to be united with him in everything in order that she, with him, may enter into the One . . ."

Irenaeus indicated he knew of Marcus' antics from the women who had returned to "the church of God" and confessed that they had loved Marcus with violent passion. The disciples of Marcus were said to have similarly deceived many women. "They claim they are in the heights beyond every power," Irenaeus said, "and as a result are free to do anything."

The story of Marcus and his lustful disciples, of course, is not from the Nag Hammadi library but from the polemics of Irenaeus. And slandering opponents, scholars say, is a well-documented way of refuting them.

Still, some Gnostics did have a bridal chamber ceremony. The Pleroma seemed to be the setting for the Valentinian bridal chamber described by church fathers. It is a future celestial scene in which marriages are to be performed between Sophia and Jesus and between the human spirits and their bridegrooms, the angels around Jesus. When the restoration of the Pleroma is complete, the world would then be extinguished in the fire of ignorance.

In the Nag Hammadi library, *The Exegesis on the Soul* tells of the wanderings of the female half of the soul who goes from one adultery to another. She appeals to heaven, is purified through baptism, and reunited with her male partner in a bridal chamber, and they become one in a lustless way.

The bridal chamber is mentioned prominently in Nag Hammadi's *The Gospel of Philip*. Like other Gnostic "gospels," it is not the story of Jesus' life, but commentaries on it. *Philip* bears some affinities to Valentinian thought. It may have been written about the second half of the second century in the area of Antioch, says German scholar Martin Krause.

Jesus emerges as a mystery-laden figure in *Philip*, whose author "reveals" the relative importance of the names Jesus, Christ, and Nazarene. Jesus himself appeared in different forms to different people—to the great as great, to the small as small, said *Philip*. In fact, the Lord did everything in a mysterious way, the text implies, and the Savior's work is still functioning through the sacraments.

Gnostics generally were thought to have been disinterested in the sacraments of Christian churches, but *Philip* mentions baptism, communion, anointing, and other rites—with the most important being the bridal chamber.

At times it seems that this ritual refers to an earthly marriage ceremony. *Philip* says that since Eve was separated from Adam and they became two persons, men and women have suffered death, but in marriage men and women can become united. "The mystery of marriage is great. For (through) it the world became numerous", according to Krause's translation in Werner Foerster's *Gnosis*, volume 2.

And yet *Philip* describes another, more sacred marriage. The privacy, the mystery of worldly marriage is such that no one but the man and wife know the day when they have intercourse, *Philip* declares. But if this marriage of "defilement" is hidden, "how much more is the undefiled marriage a true mystery. It is not carnal but pure. It does not belong to lust, but to the will. It does not belong to the darkness or the night, but it belongs to the day and the light."

The ritual in *Philip* apparently involves the symbolic marriage of one's spirit to its heavenly counterpart. It is a means of salvation, for *Philip* says if one becomes "a child of the bridal chamber" one receives the light. If one does not receive the sacrament on earth, one will not receive the light in the world to come.

The world changes for the initiate who has gone through the bridal chamber. "He who has the knowledge of the truth is free. But the free do not sin. For he who sins is the slave of sin," says *Philip*. "Be not afraid of the flesh, nor love it. If you are afraid of it, it will rule you; if you love it, it will swallow you up and throttle you."

That apparently evenhanded approach advised in *The Gospel of Philip* is rejected in a text more disdainful of worldly pleasures, *The Book of Thomas the Contender*. In that text Jesus says: "Woe to you who love intercourse with anything feminine and the defilement which (goes) together with it!"

In this case and others Jesus is no doubt "used" by Gnostic writers and editors as an authoritative figure to express what the Gnostics themselves believed.

The Gnostics also put words in the mouths of Jesus' followers, although some traditions about the disciples may have been followed in creating dialogues. At any rate, Mary Magdalene is pictured as loved greatly by Jesus, who revealed divine secrets to her. This is one of several indications that most Gnostics neither viewed women as sex objects nor less than equal before their God. At times, women even seemed to be more blessed.

In the Berlin Museum's *Gospel of Mary*, Peter says to Mary: "Sister, we know that the Savior loved you more than the rest of the women. Tell us the words of the Savior which you remember . . ."

Mary relates what the Savior told her and concludes with a story of how the soul safely passes by seven powers of wrath on its heavenly ascent.

When she finishes, Andrew questions whether the Savior really said that. "For certainly these teachings are strange ideas," Andrew says.

"Did he really speak privately with a woman (and) not openly with us?" Peter asks.

Breaking into tears, Mary responds: "My brother, Peter, what do you think? Do you think that I thought this up myself in my heart, or that I am lying about the Savior?"

Levi comes to Mary's defense. "Peter, you have always been hot-tempered. Now I see you contending against the woman like the adversaries. But if the Savior made her worthy, who are you indeed to reject her? Surely the Savior knows her very well. That is why he loved her more than us." Levi urges the disciples to "put on the perfect man," disperse and preach the gospel, which, according to *The Gospel of Mary*, they did.

Certain female biblical personages may come by an honored status partly because of the prominence of the Sophia myth in Gnosticism. Eve, for instance, was more than mere mortal in the Gnostic view; she was the divinely empowered daughter of Sophia.

Mary Magdalene was more than just a friend and follower of Jesus in *The Gospel of Philip*. Apparently elaborating on the Gospel of John's description of three Marys at the cross when Jesus was crucified, *Philip* hints that all three were forms of one personage: "Three were walking with the Lord always: Mary his mother and her sister and Magdalene who is called his companion. For Mary is his sister and his mother and his companion."

In another segment of *Philip*, Jesus is asked why he loved Mary so much and kissed her often. Jesus' indirect answer is that she is the manifestation of Sophia—who in Valentinianism is the companion/sister/bride-to-be of the Savior.

Mary Magdalene might seem to be given a second-rate status in *The Gospel of Thomas*. The last saying in *Thomas* says she must become a "male" to get into the kingdom of heaven.

> Simon Peter said to them: Let Mary go forth from among us, for women are not worthy of the life. Jesus said: Behold, I shall lead her, that I may make her male, in order that she may become a living spirit like you males. For every woman who makes herself male shall enter into the kingdom of heaven.

But actually, as James Brashler explains it, "to become a male" is standard (albeit "chauvinistic") language of the Hellenistic world for becoming pure, spiritual. The phrase was used also, he said, to describe what a teacher does for a student. In that context, woman is given an equal chance for salvation.

Feminists might find something more to cheer about in another part of *The Gospel of Thomas*. Some modern theologians who have argued that Jesus was a feminist have cited, among others, an exchange in Luke 11:27–28. They say this passage shows that Jesus did not regard women primarily as "baby machines."

Essentially the same exchange occurs in Thomas (No. 79).

> A woman from the multitude said to Him: Blessed is the womb which bore Thee, and the breasts which nourished Thee. He said to [her]: Blessed are those who have heard the word of the Father (and) have kept it in truth.

Then, *Thomas* has Jesus adding one more line:

> For there will be days when you will say: Blessed is the womb which has not conceived, and the breasts which have not suckled.

Luke has these same last lines but placed them later in his Gospel (23:29), just before the crucifixion.

Were they originally together as in *Thomas?* They seem logical as a unit since the last line is a direct response to the woman's remark. Feminists might find it a perfectly logical sequence as far as content, if not a prophecy for the days of women's liberation!

Undoubtedly the Gnostic myths of Sophia and her manifestation in Barbelo, Eve, Norea, and Mary Magdalene contributed to a better-than-average attitude by Gnostics toward women as worthy persons in the first centuries. It's almost a tenet of some scholars that the dominant male image of the deity in orthodox Judeo-Christian tradition contributed to the dominance of males in ordinary human affairs.

Assessment of the Gnostic attitudes toward male-female relationships—like other assessments of Gnostic opinion—is made difficult by the variety of Gnostic thought in the Nag

Hammadi library. Frederik Wisse finds that if there is any unity to the library it must be found, not in doctrine, but in the ethical stance.

An ascetic morality is preached, particularly in the non-Gnostic and marginally Gnostic tractates, Wisse says. The Gnostic God "and the pious believer are contrasted to the rest of mankind with (its) lusts and concerns of the flesh."

However, the inclusion of non-Gnostic materials supporting the ascetic viewpoint would indicate that to the collectors of the Nag Hammadi library—monks from the nearby monasteries? —such an outlook was an important criterion for what texts to retain. The Gnostics apparently wrote many treatises—not all included in the Nag Hammadi library. "It may be an accident of history that we have only documents supporting asceticism," said Birger Pearson.

NINETEEN

Gnosticism and Mockery

When a camel driver native to the Nile River region northeast of Nag Hammadi unearthed a large jar in late 1945 and discovered leather-bound codices, the light of day shone on papyrus manuscripts that had not been so exposed for nearly sixteen hundred years.

The Gnostics, lovers of the Light, had almost faded from the scene by the time the Nag Hammadi library was secreted away in the late fourth century, perhaps by monks who were not even true Gnostics. The writings, like any considered at odds with orthodox views, were ordered destroyed to stamp out undesired teachings. The church was still in its growing years struggling internally with creedal differences and externally with changing governmental reigns. Heretical interpretations were dealt with harshly, and would be for centuries to come.

The manuscripts provide the twentieth century with an unexpected look at some of the religious concepts rejected by orthodox forces, for better or worse, at a formative time in the history of Western civilization. The library also sheds more light on ideas Christianity borrowed and ideas that were radical alternatives to what became conventional Judaic and Christian thought (and therefore the moral, cultural, and intellectual roots of the West).

What of Gnosticism itself? Why didn't it survive? The

adoption of Christianity as the state religion of the Roman Empire surely was a major reason.

But there may have been some inherent weaknesses in Gnosticism, especially when compared to Christianity's strong points. Gnosticism lacked a real, historical savior figure, the likes of Jesus. Aside from the Christian's argument that, indeed, no one was comparable to the Son of God, the Gnostics did not rally round Simon Magus, his whore-companion Helena and his priests. Nor did Gnostics all flock to adopt Mani of the third century as their savior (no Manichaean texts or references are seen in the Nag Hammadi collection), though his Gnostic-like religion did make a stir for a few centuries. Many Gnostic Christians appeared, apparently those who accepted Jesus as a savior figure who was perhaps foreshadowed by such mythical Gnostic redeemers as Sophia, Derdekeas, and the Illuminator.

The Gnostic religion may have had its best chance for survival as a form of Christianity. A mild form of Gnostic expression lived in the works of Clement of Alexandria and others considered orthodox churchmen. Valentinus and his school came closest to acceptability, but failed.

Christianity tended to drive toward doctrinal unity while Gnostic thinkers apparently preferred their independent ways. They seemed to seek and incorporate into their systems any bit of "truth" or "knowledge" they found, regardless of the source.

Who were the Gnostics? They may have arisen among Jews, whether they were Jewish themselves or not. But if there was any ethnic or racial core at the beginning, surely they were as diverse as Christians by the second century and living in widely spread parts of the Mediterranean lands.

Robinson has called them the "dropouts" of that era. A feeling of helplessness swept over many people under the awesome power of the Roman Empire, and Gnosticism is said to have radically met the demand for a religion that declared, in effect, "Stop the world, I want to get off." The Gnostics considered the world and its creator to be evil, that a higher Father of truth exists, and that a spark of him resides in every person. Knowing this and knowing all the other secrets of mankind's origin and fate is the way of salvation.

Together with this picture of the Gnostics is one of indulgence in "gleefully shocking blasphemy," as Jonas put it. The mocking laughter of the Gnostics can be traced throughout the Nag Hammadi library. Though this is a subjective judgment, it seems at times that the more Gnostic the text, the more audible the laughter.

Mockery may be a trait common to all new and struggling religious movements—especially those which feel particularly alienated from society or conventional religious expressions. The laughter serves as an answer for the ridicule of outsiders and as a way of supporting one another—laughing at the ignorant opposition.

The nature of laughter as it appears in Gnostic writings might be divided into three, admittedly speculative stages of the religion's rise and fall—the bitter beginnings immersed in sarcasm, the occasional periods of success that bring joy, and the losing battles which invite the scorn of outsiders.

The mocking Wisdom figure of Proverbs was seen as the laughing Sophia and the laughing Eve in the presumably early works such as *The Nature of the Archons, On the Origin of the World*, and *The Apocryphon of John.*

In the second stage, the laughing Jesus mocks his would-be persecutors from above the cross, but his mocking laughter is mixed "with joy." In some texts, Jesus is described as laughing merrily with his disciples. According to Irenaeus, a Valentinian version of the Sophia myth had linked Sophia's laughter with the Light—the only happy moments in the myth of progressive error. This was the occasionally successful period of Gnosticism.

As Gnostic beliefs came under the heels of Christian orthodoxy, however, the Gnostics learned that mockery was a two-way street. A missionary religious group by this time, Gnostics found that their unconventional beliefs would be met, not only by the disinterested doubter, but also by the mocking unbeliever. As Thomas says imploringly to Jesus in *The Book of Thomas the Contender*, a text which may have been written in the early third century, "But these words that you speak to us are laughing-stocks to the world and sneered at, since they are misunderstood. So how can we go preach to them . . . ?"

In the New Testament, Jesus does not laugh, and only Luke's Gospel mentions Jesus' talking about laughter. In Luke's "Sermon on the Plain" (chap. 6), Jesus says, "Blessed are you that weep now, for you shall laugh," and later, "Woe to you that laugh now, for you shall mourn and weep." It would seem that he is referring to the change the believer will undergo, laughing for joy when experiencing the kingdom of heaven. Those who continue to reject Jesus' proclamation of the kingdom of heaven and laugh at the concept will find themselves mourning the day.

The Apostle Paul cautioned the Galatians (6:7): "Do not be deceived; God is not mocked, for whatever a man sows, that he will also reap."

Indeed, the Gnostics did reap the mockery they sowed. But wasn't their cultivation of radically different religious concepts a contribution to the creative religious climate of the first centuries? Wasn't Western civilization poorer for the loss of the Gnostic writing, imbued as they were with provocative religious imagery?

A brooding and brilliant intellectual of the turn of the last century, Frederich Nietzsche, chafed under the monotheistic ideal of Western civilization's Judeo-Christian heritage and ridiculed the hold it had on creative thinking. "Monotheism . . . the rigid consequence of the doctrine of one normal human being—consequently the belief in a normal God, beside whom there are only false, spurious Gods—has perhaps been the greatest danger of mankind in the past," Nietzsche once wrote. "In polytheism man's free-thinking and many-sided thinking has a prototype set up: the power to create for himself new and individual eyes, always newer and more individualized."

Nietzsche wrote in *Thus Spake Zarathustra* that the old gods came to an end long ago. "One day they laughed themselves to death," he said. "That happened when the most godless word issued from one of the gods themselves—the word: 'There is one god. Thou shalt have no other god before me!' "

APPENDIX

The Nag Hammadi Gnostic Library

The subject matter and nature of each tractate is indicated in brief descriptions by James Brashler of the Institute for Antiquity and Christianity, Claremont, Calif. The codex number is in Roman numerals, the tractate number in Arabic numerals.

I

1 The Apocryphon of James This secret writing describes a revelation given to the apostle James by the Savior after the resurrection. After teachings about the crucifixion, faith, the soul, prophecy, and knowledge—all from a decidedly Gnostic viewpoint—the Savior departs and James returns to Jerusalem.

2 The Gospel of Truth An unnamed Gnostic teacher enigmatically expounds the hidden mystery of Jesus, the Christ, who was crucified for those whose names are inscribed in the living book of the living and who reveals the knowledge that enables the Gnostic to escape the illusory world of ignorance vividly described as a terrible dream.

3 The Treatise on the Resurrection Addressed to an inquirer, Rheginos, this tightly reasoned defense of the spiritual reality of the resurrection includes the invitation to "come away from the divisions and chains, and already you have the resurrection."

4 The Tripartite Tractate A rambling and sometimes muddled collection of observations from a Christian Gnostic perspective on spiritual reality, the creation of the human race, and the three-fold division of spiritual, psychic, and material beings. This long, didactic treatise is said to reflect teaching of the oriental Valentinian school of Gnostics.

5 Prayer of the Apostle Paul By means of standard liturgical formulas of Christian prayer that reflect New Testament language, this pseudonymous Gnostic writing places a request for the salvation of his "Soul of light" on the lips of the Apostle Paul.

II

1 The Apocryphon of John The entire spiritual world from the ineffable supreme Being to the three hundred and sixty five angels and the chief evil archon Ialdabaoth are described in this Barbelo Gnostic interpretation of the opening chapters of the book of Genesis. Reaction to Jewish scriptures can be seen in the recurring phrase ". . . not as Moses said."

2 The Gospel of Thomas A collection of sayings attributed to the living Jesus. Many of them closely resemble words of Jesus found in the canonical gospels, while others are previously unknown sayings.

3 The Gospel of Philip A collage of aphoristic statements with frequent parallels to Valentinian Gnostic doctrine. Especially significant are the references to sacraments including the rite of the heavenly bridal chamber.

4 The Nature of the Archons This mythological revelation discourse is linked with Sethian Gnostic views of the origin of the world and the salvation of the Sethians.

5 On the Origin of the World A parallel account to *The Nature of the Archons* (II, *4*), this mythological reinterpretation of the origin of man and the world, includes what some scholars consider the pre-Christian views of a savior-revealer and an apocalyptic conclusion that foresees the restoration of reality to its root in a world of light.

6 The Exegesis on the Soul This graphic portrayal of the fall, degradation, and redemption of a female figure linked with the soul is developed in terms of quotations from the Old and New Testaments and Homer.

7 The Book of Thomas the Contender This dialogue between the risen Jesus and Judas Thomas on eschatological and ethical themes contains vivid word pictures of the torments of hell and sharp condemnation of bestial behavior.

III

1 The Apocryphon of John A shorter version of II, *1*, also found in the Berlin Museum.

2 The Gospel of the Egyptians Not a gospel in the traditional sense, this mythological treatise of Sethian origins includes Gnostic hymns, prayers and incantations of a highly esoteric nature.

3 Eugnostos, the Blessed The unknowable highest God, the androgynous primal man, the Son of Man, and the heavenly aeons are described in this non-Christian Gnostic cosmogony.

4 The Sophia of Jesus Christ This document appears to be a Christian version of *Eugnostos, the Blessed* in which the revealer is identified as Jesus and questions posed by his disciples are inserted into the material to form a Christian literary framework for originally non-Christian ideas.

5 The Dialogue of the Savior A rather fragmentary account of a conversation in which the Savior, Jesus, answers questions from his disciples about the origin of the universe, the nature of the heavenly world, salvation, and eschatology.

IV

1 The Apocryphon of John Another copy of the long version of this writing found also in II, *1*.

2 The Gospel of the Egyptians A duplicate of III, *2* with some textual variants.

V

1 Eugnostos, the Blessed A version very similar to III, *3*.

2 The Apocalypse of Paul The apostle Paul is led from the

third to the tenth heavens by a small child. Visions of the punishment of a wicked soul in the fourth heaven and a dialogue with an old man clothed in white and seated on a throne of light in the seventh heaven are reported in this rather fragmentary account.

3 The First Apocalypse of James A discussion between James the Just and Jesus both before and after the crucifixion of Jesus, who did not really suffer but only appeared to. Valentinian formulas and a very severely damaged section describing the death of James are also found in this Christian Gnostic tractate.

4 The Second Apocalypse of James This is a collection of hymnic and poetic statements by the redeemer (Jesus) and James, who functions as the agent of redemption for the Gnostic community he leads.

5 The Apocalypse of Adam Viewed by several scholars as an important non-Christian Gnostic writing, this document reports the pre-fall existence of Adam and Eve in paradise, their fall into ignorance, and their rescue by three men who reveal the future fate of the children of Seth. An especially interesting section describes the origin of the Illuminator by the thirteen kingdoms.

VI

1 The Acts of Peter and the Twelve Apostles This account of a sea voyage by Peter and the twelve disciples includes a meeting with a pearl peddler who turns out to be the risen Savior in disguise.

2 The Thunder: Perfect Mind A series of paradoxical self-predications uttered by a female figure are contained in this enigmatic tractate.

3 Authoritative Teaching In this Gnostic homily the situation of the soul in a hostile world of evil is described in vivid images and symbols.

4 The Concept of Our Great Power This Gnostic apocalypse, difficult to decipher, seems to present an outline of world history that includes a series of catastrophes from which the pure souls will ultimately be redeemed.

5 The Republic of Plato 588b–589b This hopelessly confused attempt to translate a summary statement from Plato's philosophical masterpiece has resulted in a nearly unrecognizable Coptic version.

6 On the Eighth and the Ninth A fascinating account of initiation into the mysteries of Hermetism is recorded in this didactic dialogue between Hermes Trismegistos and his student, who has a vision of the eighth (heaven?) that reveals the ninth (heaven?).

7 The Prayer of Thanksgiving This widely circulated prayer (Greek and Latin versions also exist) reflects cultic practices probably carried out in Hermetic communes.

8 Asclepius This Coptic version of part of a document previously preserved only in Latin and a few Greek fragments belong to the corpus of Hermetic writings. It contains an apocalyptic vision of the fate of Egypt when abandoned by the gods.

VII

1 The Paraphrase of Shem An allegorical account of the primordial events that culminated in the creation of the world, a struggle between forces of light and darkness, and the redemption of the children of Shem, the Sodomites, by a redeemer called Derdekeas.

2 The Second Treatise of the Great Seth This Christian Gnostic document dwells on the role of the redeemer in descending to the physical world to struggle with the archons and to rescue his Gnostic brothers after only appearing to die on the cross. Gnostic mythology and docetic Christology are combined with a very negative attitude toward the heroes of the Jewish Scriptures.

3 The Apocalypse of Peter The laughing Savior interprets visions seen by Peter of the persecution and apparent crucifixion of Jesus in order to strengthen him as the leader of a struggling Gnostic group opposed by bishops and deacons.

4 The Teachings of Silvanus This lengthy philosophical discourse enjoins renunciation of the physical world as the prerequisite to following the way of Christ described in typical Gnostic terms as "becoming like God."

5 The Three Steles of Seth This three-part collection of

meditative hymns to Adamas, Barbelo, and the Pre-existent one testifies to Sethian Gnostic liturgical practices.

VIII

1 Zostrianos A very fragmentary account of the revelation of Zostrianos, who is led by the angel of knowledge and others through the heavenly worlds.

2 The Letter of Peter to Philip The introductory epistle framework of this document soon gives way to a typical Gnostic revelation discourse concerning the heavenly world and the earthly life and apparent death of Jesus.

IX

1 Melchizedek This extremely fragmentary document reveals Sethian affinities and tantalizing but incomplete references to intra-Gnostic theological differences described by the figure Melchizedek known from Jewish and Christian sources.

2 The Thought of Norea This short, poetic statement apparently describes the situation of Norea in the heavenly Pleroma.

3 The Testimony of Truth A Gnostic homily addressed to those who are able to hear spiritually. The unnamed author attacks orthodox Christians as well as other Gnostic groups as he sets forth "the true testimony."

X

1 Marsanes This very badly damaged codex once contained an elaborate description of the heavenly world and an account of the kinds of souls in technical linguistic terms said to be "the language of the angels."

XI

1 The Interpretation of Knowledge This sermon with many Pauline and Valentinian echoes teaches its hearers to "rejoice joyfully and partake of grace."

2 A Valentinian Exposition The mysteries of Valentinian

Gnostic sacraments and a detailed description of the heavenly hierarchy are included in this tractate to which are added five cultic appendices closely related to Valentinian worship.

3 Allogenes Allogenes, "stranger," in dialogue with his son Messos gives "primary revelation of the Unknown."

4 Hypsiphrone This short revelation discourse is too badly mutilated to determine its contents.

XII

1 The Sentences of Sextus A Coptic translation of Greek ethical maxims attributed to the philosopher Sextus.

2 The Gospel of Truth A short fragment of the same document preserved in I, 2.

3 (unidentified fragments)

XIII

1 Trimorphic Protennoia Self-descriptions in the first person of a female figure, Protennoia, who then reveals a series of heavenly beings including a Gnostic redeemer.

2 On the Origin of the World A short section from the beginning of the same treatise also found in II, 5.

Note: The first 11 codices had leather covers. Codex XII consists of only 16 pages, the rest having disappeared following the 1945 discovery. Codex XIII also has only 16 pages; they were ripped out in the fourth century and were slipped into another codex.

The Berlin Museum owns four Coptic treatises, discovered in 1896 and finally published in the 1950s, which are often used for comparison with the Nag Hammadi collection at the Cairo Coptic Museum. Given the number BG 8502, the codex includes four tractates: 1, *The Gospel of Mary*; 2, *The Apocryphon of John*; 3, *The Sophia of Jesus Christ*; 4, *The Acts of Peter*.

ANNOTATED
BIBLIOGRAPHY

English Translations

Here are some of the books and journals which contain English translations of the Nag Hammadi texts:

James M. Robinson (ed.), *The Coptic Gnostic Library: Edited with an English Translation, Introductions and Notes* (Leiden: E. J. Brill, 1975–). The only complete edition of the Nag Hammadi codices plus the four texts in the Berlin Museum. The first of 11 volumes to appear was *The Gospel of the Egyptians* by Alexander Bohlig and Frederik Wisse in cooperation with Pahor Labib.

Werner Foerster (ed.), *Gnosis, a Selection of Gnostic Texts*, trans. ed. by R. McL. Wilson (Oxford: At the Clarendon Press). Vol. I, 1972, *Patristic Evidence*. Excerpts from church fathers' descriptions of Gnostics, plus *The Apocryphon of John* (Berlin copy). Vol. II, 1974, *Coptic and Mandean Sources*. Contains contributions by Martin Krause of translations of *The Apocalypse of Adam, The Letter of Eugnostos, The Hypostasis of the Archons, The Gospel of Truth, The Treatise on the Resurrection, The Gospel of Philip, The Exegesis on the Soul,* and *The Book of Thomas* (*the Athlete*).

Robert Haardt, *Gnosis: Character and Testimony*, trans. by J. F. Hendry (Leiden: E. J. Brill, 1971). Contains *The Gospel of Truth, The Treatise on the Resurrection,* and *The Gospel according to Thomas;* excerpts from *The Gospel according to Philip, On the Origin of the World,* and *The Apocryphon of John* (Berlin copy).

Kendrick Grobel, *The Gospel of Truth: A Valentinian Meditation on the Gospel. Translation from the Coptic and Commentary* (Nashville and New York: Abingdon Press, 1960).

Malcolm L. Peel, *The Epistle to Rheginos: A Valentinian Letter on the Resurrection. Introduction, Translation, Analysis, and Exposition* (Philadelphia: Westminster Press, 1969).

Roger A. Bullard, *The Hypostasis of the Archons: The Coptic Text with Translation and Commentary. With a Contribution by M. Krause* (Berlin: Walter de Gruyter, 1970).

Robert M. Grant, with David N. Freedman, *The Secret Sayings of*

Jesus with an English Translation of the Gospel of Thomas by *W. R. Schoedel* (Garden City, N.Y.: Doubleday, 1960).

Robert McL. Wilson, *The Gospel of Philip: Translated from the Coptic Text with an Introduction and Commentary* (New York and Evanston: Harper & Row, 1962).

A. Guillaumont, H.-Ch. Puech, G. Quispel, W. Till, and Y. Abd al Masih, *The Gospel according to Thomas: Coptic Text Established and Translated* (New York: Harper and Brothers, 1959).

M. Malinine, H.-Ch. Puech, G. Quispel, W. Till, R. Kasser, R. McL. Wilson, and J. Zandee, *Epistula Jacobi Apocrypha: Codex Jung F.I^r-F. VIII^v* (Zurich and Stuttgart: Rascher Verlag, 1968). Contains French, English, and German translation of *The Apocryphon of James.*

S. Kent Brown and C. Wilfred Griggs, "The Apocalypse of Peter: Introduction and Translation," *BYU Studies* (Winter 1975).

Bentley Layton, "The Hypostasis of the Archons, or the Reality of the Rulers," *Harvard Theological Review* (October 1974).

Special Reference Books

Photographs of the manuscript pages and fragments are in *The Facsimile Edition of the Nag Hammadi Codices* (Leiden: E. J. Brill). Codex VI, 1972; Codex VII, 1972; Codices XI, XII and XIII, 1973; Codex II, 1974; Codex V, 1975; Codex IV, 1975; Codex III, 1976. (Edition will total 11 volumes.) Sponsored by the Arab Republic of Egypt and UNESCO, the volumes contain brief prefaces by James M. Robinson.

Excerpts and full translations of the range of Christian apocryphal writings, including some Nag Hammadi texts, are in Edgar Hennecke-Wilhelm Schneemelcher (ed.), *New Testament Apocrypha*, trans. ed. by R. McL. Wilson (Philadelphia: Westminster Press). Vol. I, 1963, *Gospels and Related Writings;* Vol. II, 1965, *Writings Relating to the Apostles; Apocalypses and Related Subjects.*

Indispensable for Gnostic studies is David M. Scholer, *Nag Hammadi Bibliography 1948–1969* (Leiden: E. J. Brill, 1971). The bibliography is updated annually in the autumn issue of the journal *Novum Testamentum.*

Special Sources for This Book

Werner Foerster's previously cited *Gnosis: A Selection of Gnostic Texts*, Vol. I, was the source in every case for quotations from church fathers.

Jean Doresse's book, *The Secret Books of the Egyptian Gnostics: An Introduction to the Gnostic Coptic Manuscripts discovered at*

Chenoboskion; With an English Translation and Critical Evaluation of the Gospel according to Thomas, trans. by P. Mairet (New York: Viking Press, 1960), was a basic source for the first few chapters. Doresse added some details for me in correspondence dated Oct. 19, 1974; July 17, 1975, and Sept. 8, 1975.

James M. Robinson's research provided many details for Part I. The information came from interviews 1973–75 and from his published works, including "The Coptic Gnostic Library Today," *New Testament Studies* 14 (1967–68), reprinted as Occasional Paper 1 of The Institute for Antiquity and Christianity; *The Facsimile Edition of the Nag Hammadi Codices: Introduction* (Leiden: E. J. Brill, 1972), reprinted as Occasional Paper 4 of The Institute for Antiquity and Christianity, and *The Nag Hammadi Codices: A general introduction to the nature and significance of the Coptic Gnostic Codices from Nag Hammadi* (Claremont, Calif: The Institute for Antiquity and Christianity, 1974). The latter paperback booklet was also quoted in other parts of this book.

Books

Ugo Bianchi (ed.), *Le Origini Dello Gnosticismo: Colloquio di Messina, 13–18 Aprile 1966* (Leiden: E. J. Brill, 1970).

Bruce Bohle (ed.), *The Home Book of American Quotations* (New York: Dodd, Mead & Co., 1967).

Rudolf Bultmann, *Primitive Christianity in Its Contemporary Setting,* trans. by R. H. Fuller (Cleveland: World Publishing, Living Age/Meridian paperback, 1956).

C. W. Ceram, *Gods, Graves, and Scholars* (New York: Alfred A. Knopf, 1951, rev. ed., 1967).

Martin A. Cohen, "As Jewish History," *The Bible in Modern Scholarship,* J. Philip Hyatt (ed.) (Nashville and New York: Abingdon, 1965).

Frank L. Cross (ed.), *The Jung Codex, a newly recovered Gnostic papyrus; three studies* (London: Mowbray; New York: Morehouse-Gorham, 1955).

Robert M. Grant, "Gnosticism," *Encyclopedia Britannica Macropaedia* (Chicago: Encyclopedia Britannica, 1974).

———, *Gnosticism and Early Christianity* (New York and London: Columbia University Press, 1959, first ed.; 1966, second ed.).

Robert Graves and Raphael Patai, *Hebrew Myths: The Book of Genesis* (New York: McGraw-Hill Book Co., paperback, 1966).

A. K. Helmbold, *The Nag Hammadi Gnostic Texts and the Bible* (Grand Rapids: Baker, 1967).

R. Travers Herford, *Pirke Aboth, The Ethics of the Talmud: Sayings of the Fathers, Text, Complete Translation and Commentaries (New York: Schocken Books, 1962).

Hans Jonas, "Response to G. Quispel's 'Gnosticism and the New Testament,'" *The Bible in Modern Scholarship*. See also, Robert McL. Wilson's response in same book, previously cited.

——, *The Gnostic Religion: The Message of the Alien God and the Beginnings of Christianity* (Boston: Beacon Press, 1958; second paperback edition, 1963).

Carl G. Jung, *Memories, Dreams, Reflections*, recorded and edited by Aniela Jaffe (New York: Pantheon, 1961).

——, *The Collected Works of C. G. Jung*, trans. by R. F. C. Hull, vol. 9, part II (New York: Pantheon, 1959).

Friedrich Nietzsche, "The Greatest Utility of Polytheism," in *Joyful Wisdom*, trans. by Thomas Common (New York: Ungar Publishing Co., 1960) and *Thus Spake Zarathustra*, trans. by Walter Kaufmann (New York: Viking Press, 1966)—as quoted in David L. Miller, *The New Polytheism* (New York: Harper & Row, 1974).

Birger A. Pearson, "Jewish Haggadic Traditions in *The Testimony of Truth* (CG IX, 3)," *Ex Orbe Religionum: Studia Geo Widengren* (Lugduni Batavorum: E. J. Brill, 1972).

——, "Nag Hammadi Codices," *1974 Yearbook of the Encyclopedia Judaica* (Jerusalem: Keter Publishing House, 1974).

——, "Anti-Heretical Warnings in Codex IX from Nag Hammadi," *Essays on the Nag Hammadi Text in Honor of Pahor Labib*, Martin Krause (ed.) (Leiden: E. J. Brill, 1975).

Norman Perrin, *Rediscovering the Teaching of Jesus* (New York and Evanston: Harper & Row, 1967).

Gilles Quispel, "Gnosticism and the New Testament," *The Bible in Modern Scholarship*.

——, "The Origins of the Gnostic Demiurge," *Kyriakon: Festschrift Johannes Quasten*, P. Granfield and J. A. Jungmann (ed.) (Munster: Aschendorff, 1970).

James M. Robinson and Helmut Koester, *Trajectories through Early Christianity* (Philadelphia: Fortress Press, 1971).

David Syme Russell, *The Method and Message of Jewish Apocalyptic 200 BC–AD 100* (Philadelphia: Westminster, 1964).

Gershom Scholem, *Major Trends in Jewish Mysticism* (New York: Schocken Books (paperback), 1961).

Robert McL. Wilson, *Gnosis and the New Testament* (Philadelphia: Fortress Press, 1968).

Orval Wintermute, "A Study of Gnostic Exegesis of the Old Testament," *The Use of the Old Testament in the New and Other Essays: Studies in Honor of William Franklin Stinespring*, J. M. Efird (ed.) (Durham: Duke University Press, 1972).

Yigael Yadin, *The Message of the Scrolls* (New York: Simon and Schuster, 1957).

Edwin M. Yamauchi, *Pre-Christian Gnosticism: A Survey of the Proposed Evidences* (Grand Rapids: Eerdmans, 1973).

Essays on the Coptic Gnostic Library (Leiden: E. J. Brill, 1970). This paperback off-print contains five articles from the journal *Novum Testamentum* XII (1970): George MacRae, "The Jewish Background of the Gnostic Sophia Myth;" William C. Robinson Jr., "The Exegesis on the Soul;" William R. Schoedel, "Scripture and the Seventy-two Heavens of the First Apocalypse of James;" Frederik Wisse, "The Redeemer Figure in the Paraphrase of Shem," and Malcolm L. Peel, "Gnostic Eschatology and the New Testament."

Journals

Jean Doresse, "A Gnostic Library from Upper Egypt," *Archeology* (Summer 1950).

Soren Giversen, "The Apocryphon of John and Genesis," *Studia Theologia* 17 (1963).

Robert M. Grant, "Gnostic Origins and the Basilideans of Irenaeus," *Vigiliae Christianae* 13 (1959).

George E. Ladd, "The Search for Perspective," *Interpretation: A Journal of Bible and Theology* XXV (Jan. 1971).

George MacRae, "Biblical News: Gnosis in Messina," *Catholic Biblical Quarterly*, XXVIII (1966).

———, "The Coptic Gnostic Apocalypse of Adam," *The Heythrop Journal* 6 (1965).

Ralph Marcus, "Pharisees, Essenes, and Gnostics," *Journal of Biblical Literature* 73 (1954).

Jacob Neusner, " 'Pharisaic-Rabbinic' Judaism: A Clarification," *History of Religions* (Feb. 1973).

Birger A. Pearson, "Friedlander Revisited: Alexandrian Judaism and Gnostic Origins," *Studia Philonica* II (1973).

Frederik Wisse, "The Nag Hammadi Library and the Heresiologists," *Vigiliae Christianae* 25 (1971).

Jan Zandee, "Gnostic Ideas on the Fall and Salvation," *Numen* 11 (1964).

Newspapers

John Dart, "Serpent Plays the Hero's Role in the Gnostic Garden of Eden," *Los Angeles Times*, Sept. 9, 1973.

Andrew M. Greeley, "A Christmas Biography," *New York Times Magazine*, Dec. 23, 1973.

Dan L. Thrapp, "Letter Tells of Risen Christ's Unrecorded Visit,

Coptic Document Found in Egypt Rivals Dead Sea Scrolls, Claremont Scholar Says," *Los Angeles Times*, July 13, 1966.

"New Light on a Coptic Codex: 'Gospel of Truth,'" *London Times*, Nov. 16, 1953.

Papers Delivered in Academic Circles

James Brashler, "The Apocalypse of Peter," paper at the Nag Hammadi seminar, the Society of Biblical Literature, Oct. 26, 1974, Washington, D.C.

Joseph A. Gibbons, "A Commentary on *The Second Logos of the Great Seth*," Ph.D. dissertation, Yale University, 1972.

George MacRae, "Discourses of the Gnostic Revealer," paper delivered at the International Congress on Gnosticism, Stockholm, 1973.

———, "*The Apocalypse of Adam* Reconsidered," the Society of Biblical Literature Proceedings, Vol. II, Sept. 1–5, 1972, Los Angeles.

Birger A. Pearson, "Biblical Exegesis in Gnostic Literature," unpublished paper.

———, "The Figure of Norea in Gnostic Literature," paper at the International Congress on Gnosticism, Stockholm, 1973.

Pheme Perkins, "Hiding in Sheol: Theophany of the Divine Warrior and the Appearance of the Gnostic Revealer in Chaos," paper at the Catholic Biblical Assn. Task Force on Apocalyptic, Chicago, August 1974.

———, "Peter in Gnostic Revelation," the Society of Biblical Literature 1974 Seminar Papers, Vol. II, October 24, 1974, Washington, D.C.

Gilles Quispel, "Jung and the Jung Codex," paper at the Panarion Conference, Los Angeles, Sept. 5, 1975.

James M. Robinson, "Jewish Gnostic Nag Hammadi Texts," Protocol of the Third Colloquy of the Center for Hermeneutical Studies in Hellenistic and Modern Culture, Berkeley, Calif., May 22, 1972.

Frederik Wisse, "The Sethians and the Nag Hammadi Library," the Society of Biblical Literature Proceedings, Vol. II, Sept. 1–5, 1972, Los Angeles.

W. Wuellner (ed.), "The Thunder: Perfect Mind," Protocol of the Fifth Colloquy of the Center for Hermeneutical Studies in Hellenistic and Modern Culture, Berkeley, Calif., March 11, 1973.

INDEX